# Z E N

## IN 10 SIMPLE LESSONS

# Z E N

## IN 10 SIMPLE LESSONS

**ANTHONY MAN-TU LEE and DAVID WEISS**

First edition for the United States and
its territories published exclusively by
Barron's Education Services, Inc. in 2002.

DESIGNER  Jane Lanaway
ILLUSTRATORS  Rhian Nest James, Trina Dalziel
PHOTOGRAPHY  Ian Parsons
CALLIGRAPHY  Hiroshi Ueta

*All inquiries should be addressed to:*
Barron's Educational Series, Inc.
250 Wireless Boulevard
Hauppauge, NY 11788
**http://www.barronseduc.com**

Library of Congress Catalog Card No. 00-108530
International Standard Book No. 0-7641-1835-8

PRINTED IN CHINA BY HONG KONG GRAPHICS AND PRINTING

9 8 7 6 5 4 3 2 1

# Contents

前言

# Introduction

We talk of "Zen gardening" and "Zen jogging"; we have *Zen and the Art of Web Design* and *Zen and the Art of Motorcycle Maintenance*. The word "Zen" has come to symbolize many things in our culture: simplicity; austerity; directness; efficiency. Zen embodies all these things—but much more besides. Zen is in danger of becoming debased; its very popularity is dangerous.

If you are a fan of Akira Kurosawa's movie *The Seven Samurai* or of James Clavell's novel *Shogun*, you may be dimly aware of the role that Zen has played in Japanese history. Or you may have heard about its role in the work of Jack Kerouac. Zen has influenced many cultures and inspired great works of art, but there is more to Zen than samurai and Beat poetry. So what is Zen all about then? Is it a religion? Is it a philosophy? Is it a cult? Can you "do" Zen? And what's all this you've heard about "Enlightenment?"

*Zen in 10 Simple Lessons* is our attempt to help you dip your toe in the water, so that you can experience a little bit of Zen. It is really all about experience: how you experience your life, interpret it, and react to it. Zen has been called "direct knowledge" because it can cut through the smokescreen of the everyday and straight to the heart of reality.

Zen thrives on paradox. The more you "think" about it, the less you will really understand. The more you try to seek "Enlightenment," the further you will get from it. For those of you used to Western modes of logic, be prepared to struggle.

**Below** The Ox symbolizes enlightenment. It is a wild, difficult ride—whose purpose is to forget the Ox altogether!

Zen is not logical, as you understand the term. If this annoys or scares you, then Zen is not for you.

Millions of people around the world practice Zen in one form or another. For some, it is merely a way to relax and enjoy life more fully; for others, it is a deadly serious struggle to achieve oneness with the Buddha and with all things. Some people drift in and out of practice; others spend a great deal of their time in temples and retreats. The great thing about Zen is that, being fundamentally nonjudgmental, it allows you to choose your own level of practice without the burden of feeling guilty or sinful. *Zen in 10 Simple Lessons* is aimed at those who are interested in a Zen way of life and the trappings of a Zen lifestyle, but a book like this cannot pretend to cover all the nuances and facets of this very complex subject.

Zen has flourished in numerous countries and cultures. Many Zen practitioners in North America and Europe follow Chinese, Korean, Vietnamese, or Japanese Zen *roshi* (teachers). Our view of Zen is based on our experience of it—which is that of casual practitioners from North America who know about Zen mainly through its Japanese lineage. If, by the end of this book, you wish to delve more deeply into the subject, there is a list of web sites and books for further reading that will feed your growing hunger. Meanwhile, sit down in a comfortable position with your back straight, begin counting your breath, and start searching for the ox.

**Above** The Laughing Buddha was a mendicant monk who roamed the countryside in the Daoist tradition helping others. He is revered as an incarnation of Maitreya, the Buddha of the Future. A sixteenth-century limestone relief from Lingyin Temple in Hangzhou, China.

" *Zen is like looking for the spectacles that are sitting on your nose.* "

UNATTRIBUTED

# 1 The Origins of Zen

Zen is a school of Buddhism, which is based on the teachings of the Prince Siddhartha Gautama during the sixth century B.C.E. Pythagoras, Zoroaster, and Confucius were his contemporaries.

## The Buddha

Siddhartha was born in the Indian kingdom of Kapalivastu, and his father was told by an oracle that his son would become a great spiritual teacher. Since this was not part of the father's dynastic plans, he kept Siddhartha shielded from all knowledge of poverty, sadness, sickness, aging, and death by immersing him in the luxurious life of the court. Like many parental plans, this one unraveled. At the age of 29 the young prince looked down from the ramparts of the castle where he was secluded and saw an aged man, a sick man, and a corpse. These sights brought home to Siddhartha that suffering is the lot of the vast majority of mankind.

Siddhartha was so distraught that he fled his father's palace and began a spiritual journey that consumed the rest of his life. He became obsessed by the nature of human suffering: what caused it; why it existed; whether it could be overcome. In trying to answer these burning questions, he

> *The temple bell stops but the sound keeps coming out of the flowers.*
>
> BASHO, ZEN POET
> 1644–1694 C.E.

joined a group of ascetics living in a nearby forest. This did not, however, bring him the spiritual solace he sought. Finally he decided that he would sit down and would not move until he had figured it all out by himself. He sat beneath a *bodhi* tree by a river (near present-day Bodh Gaya) and spent six years pondering his experiences. During this time, like many other spiritual seekers, he was tempted by visions of immense riches, fleshly delights, and false enlightenment.

At last he experienced an intense awakening—so intense that it almost killed him on the spot. This was (and is) the Great Enlightenment, or *satori* (Awakening), which Zen claims to transmit. "Wonder of wonders!" he is reported to have exclaimed (according to the *Kegon Sutra*), "Intrinsically all living beings are Buddhas, endowed with wisdom and virtue, but because men's minds have become inverted through delusive thinking, they fail to perceive this."

From that time on Siddhartha became known as the Buddha (the Enlightened One), or the Tathagatha (He Who Has Traveled Forward and Returned). He spent the remaining 45 years of his life traveling up and down the Indian subcontinent, trying to share with others the *dharma* (truth) that he had experienced. His lectures were often wordless, for he claimed that the dharma was beyond words. Much of the earliest surviving Buddhist literature was actually written down by his successors, who, driven by an eagerness to share, dredged their own memories for the Buddha's lectures and dialogs. Many of these texts are known as *sutras*, and were written in Pali and Sanskrit (ancient Indo-Aryan languages). To this day they are chanted by Buddhists worldwide—not because they are laws to be memorized and followed blindly, but because they embody wisdom and, as such, are worth listening to (even when untranslated).

**Left** The Buddhist image of a lotus rising from the mud of a pond or lake derived from Hindu symbolism of the cycle of reincarnation, blooming, and then returning to the mud from which it grew. Lotus ponds are frequently found within the grounds of Buddhist temples.

**Far left** Amida, the Buddha of the Western Paradise, is considered an emanation of Siddhartha in contemplation with hands in the *dhyanamudra* (gesture of meditation). This small bronze is a copy of the Daibutsu at Kamakura, the original center of Zen in Japan.

## The Transmission

One day near the end of his life, the Buddha was lecturing from a mountainside called Vulture Peak to a throng of disciples below. He often used nontraditional methods of conveying his message. On this day he wordlessly held up a large flower. At that moment one person in the multitude, by the name of Maha-kashyapa, immediately experienced the same Awakening that the Buddha had experienced many years before, and smiled. Because of his own heightened awareness, the Buddha instantly recognized the change in Maha-kashyapa, even from a distance. Maha-kashyapa was to become the driving force in the continuation of the Buddha's ideas, and modern-day Zen claims its legitimacy through this "Transmission" from the Buddha to Maha-kashyapa. He in turn transmitted the dharma through a series of patriarchs, or founding fathers.

**Left** Flowers in Buddhism represent a virtuous form produced from the union of innate reason and knowledge. The lotus is the most honored as a symbol of reincarnation.

**Below** The Buddha often lectured wordlessly, believing that words often intervened between seekers and the truth. Here he holds up a flower to the multitude; only one man understood, became his disciple, and began the Zen lineage.

## From India to China

The first 28 patriarchs of Zen Buddhism came from the Indian subcontinent. Around 520 C.E. the 28th patriarch, Bodhidharma, traveled to China to spread the dharma, although Amidist and other schools of Buddhism had already been established there. Bodhidharma settled at the Shao-lin Temple in northern China and spent nine years attaining Enlightenment. His disciple, Hui Ke (487–593 C.E.), became the first Chinese patriarch.

Bodhidharma and Hui Ke are the subjects of many legends, artworks, and poetry. Hui Ke was a scholar of repute who had heard of Buddhism and the peace of mind that it supposedly brought. He traveled to see Bodhidharma to ask how he, too, could achieve this state of mind. Bodhidharma repeatedly turned Hui Ke away, saying that seeking Enlightenment was not for the fainthearted. Finally, after hours of standing in the snow, Hui Ke cut off his left arm and threw it at Bodhidharma's feet, convincing him of his serious intentions.

Zen Buddhism successfully took root in China, though not without being affected by the new soil that was nurturing it. Two Chinese philosophies—Daoism and Confucianism—influenced the growth and change of *Chan* (the Chinese transliteration of the Sanskrit word *dhyana*), as Bodhidharma's brand of Buddhism came to be called.

The last Chinese patriarch, Huineng (638–713 c.e.), was born a peasant and, like all truly free spirits, paid little heed to following the prescribed forms. He was desperately poor as a young man and worked as a common laborer. He apparently attained Enlightenment upon first hearing the *Diamond Sutra* (one of the most important Buddhist texts) read to him. Because he had not come up through the established hierarchy (and even Buddhists have a hard time shaking off jealousy and prejudice), he was not esteemed by his fellows. On the death of the previous patriarch, Hongren, however, it was Huineng who was appointed in his place.

Huineng is a pivotal figure because he was the first patriarch to practice Zen outside the umbrella of Indian culture, and many of his teachings and writings have been preserved. He never formally passed on the patriarchy and thus the official title died with him, but his successors carried on in his spirit.

## Daoism and Confucianism

Daoism is the religion that sprang up around a book called the *Dao Dejing*, which was written—according to legend—by Laozi sometime during the fifth century B.C.E. Confucianism is a school of moral and religious philosophy founded by Confucius, or Kong Fuzi (551–479 B.C.E.), whose writings include the *Analects*, *Odes*, and *Rights*.

**Right** Despite his poor upbringing and illiteracy, Huineng (638–713 C.E.) was appointed successor to the Chinese patriarch, Hongren. The fact that he was illiterate made him an unpopular choice with other monks at first, but under Huineng's guidance, Buddhism in China was able to break away from its Indian origins.

## From China to Japan

Buddhism—and Zen—continued to spread throughout the Far East. Seekers from many nations now came to China to learn about the dharma. In the late eighth century C.E. Kobo-daishi (considered the creator of written Japanese script and calligraphy) came from Japan, returning to his native land with not only a knowledge of Shingon Buddhism (esoteric Buddhism), but also a love of Chinese art and culture that was to have a huge effect on Japan. In the twelfth century Eisai Myo-an, who had trained at Mount Hiei, Japan's biggest Buddhist "university," went to China and returned with Zen and the first tea seeds, making him a doubly legendary figure. Thenceforth tea, and the ceremony that subsequently grew up around its enjoyment, became intimately entwined with Zen. Japan no longer looked to China for spiritual guidance, but established its own Zen tradition—the word Zen itself being the Japanese pronunciation of Chan.

**Above** Enlightenment seeks to end the cycle of reincarnation that binds us to endless existences. Nirvana joins beings with all that there is, like a drop of water returning to the ocean.

### Some major figures from Japanese Zen

**DOGEN** (1200–1253): founder of the Soto school, although he disavowed the concept of separate Zen schools; his prime teaching method was *shikan-taza* (following the breath, *see* Chapter 3).

**BASSUI** (1327–1387): a major Zen master, who was renowned for his *koan* "Who is the Master?"

**SESSHU** (1420–1506): a Zen monk and the finest painter of the Japanese Zen tradition.

**BASHO** (1644–1694): a Zen poet responsible for turning the *haiku* into an art form.

## Japan and Zen

From the twelfth century onward, Zen began to play an ever-greater role in the life of Japan. Zen's success in that country is mainly due to its support from the *shoguns* of the Kamakura period (1189–1375). But beyond the purely spiritual realm, Zen attitudes infused themselves into Japanese literature, art, and politics—to the point where today, in the minds of Westerners, Zen is more closely associated with Japanese culture than with any other culture.

Japanese-born Zen masters such as Dogen and Bassui produced voluminous works, which live on in translated stories and riddles. Aside from strictly spiritual texts, books such as the mendicant balladeers' *Heike mono-gatari (The Tale of the Heike)*, Kamo no Chomei's *Hojoki (An Account of My Hut)*, and Yoshida Kenko's *Tsurezuregusa (Essays in Idleness)* were inspired by the austere, down-to-earth, and direct prose that emanated from Zen teachings. A new type of poetry, *haiku*, emerged, which also drew from the Zen well. In just 17 syllables over three lines, haiku poems were evocative and poignant; in much the same way Zen masters used *koans* (riddles) in order to help adherents cut the bonds of logic and perceive reality directly.

One of the most famous haiku (*see* Chapter 9) is by Basho:

> *The ancient pond, ah...*
> *A frog ready to jump in*
> *The sound of water.*

As you will see later, much of Japanese art during the period between 1200 and 1800 used Zen legends and themes. Sesshu, Sesson Shukei, and Jasoku are the most famous Japanese artists of this period. Calligraphy itself became an art form; some of the most beautiful and treasured relics of this period are actually letterings of Zen principles.

Three new art forms—separate and yet interlocked with each other—sprang up and flourished during this period, nurtured by Zen principles:

- gardening
- *zenga* (Zen painting)
- the tea ceremony.

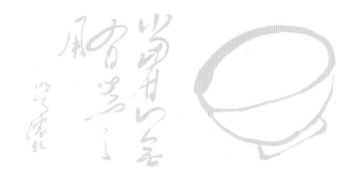

**Above** Haiku refers to both a three-line style of poetry and a simplistic, minimalist style of painting that is inspired by the poetic form. The empty bowl has associations both with the spiritual sense of the empty mind into which knowledge is poured and the more mundane reality of monastic austerity.

**Right** The symbolism of a simple poem goes further than the images described. The frog can represent single-mindedness and the solitary life—the sound of water brings to mind ripples on the water's surface, a metaphor for causation.

All emphasized the intentional blurring of the distinctions between natural and man-made materials. Zen gardens, with their raked sand, solitary stones, and composed vistas, mimicked and parodied nature at the same time. Zenga struggled to reflect natural images and figures, replacing the reliance on color with a higher regard for brush technique and subtlety of line. The tea ceremony was the most complex of all. It was an elaborate ritual that grew out of the court ceremonials in China, but metamorphosed into a uniquely Japanese artform, which drew on an appreciation of gardening, flower arrangement, calligraphy, connoisseurship, and etiquette to produce an overall effect of intense and focused casualness. If that sounds contradictory—it is. The mainspring of these contradictions was Zen.

**Above** The Zen-inspired rooms used in a tea ceremony reflect the taste of sixteenth-century tea masters such as Sen Rikyu, and reflect much of what is considered "Japanese design"—simplicity, natural building materials, minimalism, open space.

When the court-centered society in Japan gave way to the feudal system, a new class developed—the *samurai* (warrior-for-hire)—and through the patronage of the Kamakura shoguns Zen was enfolded into its *bushido,* or warrior, code (*see* Chapter 5). Just as Zen was changed in its move to China, so it changed further in its move to Japan. The continuous factional struggles of the warlords from the twelfth to the seventeenth centuries, punctuated by temporary periods of centralized power, produced a chaotic atmosphere where allegiances were always shifting. These only reinforced the Buddhist ideas that all life was change, and that permanence and attachment to permanence were illusory.

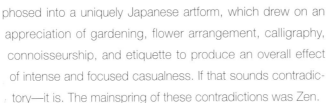

**Left** *Chabana,* or tea flowers, differs from *ikebana* (flower arrangement) in that it uses fewer and more subdued blooms, less formalized forms, and attempts to remain understated where ikebana can be bombastic.

# From Japan to the West

With the opening of Japan to the West in the mid-nineteenth century, interest in Zen Buddhism awakened in Europe and North America. Three Japanese scholars are primarily responsible for the introduction of Zen Buddhism to the West. Two of them were Zen *roshi*, or masters; one was an author with a mission.

Roshi Harada (1870–1961) was one of the first Zen masters to make a conscious effort to open Zen up to Westerners. He brought ideas of the Rinzai and Soto schools (*see* Chapter 2) together in a hybrid that was more readily accessible. His successor, Roshi Yasutani (1885–1973), continued the work, making numerous trips to North America and conferring Transmission on several American successors. Both men taught until the very end of their lives, and they can be considered to play the role in North America that Bodhidharma had played spreading the dharma in China.

But many North Americans who had never in their lives met a Zen master learned about Zen through Daisetz Suzuki (1870–1957), the first author to translate the works of Zen into English and interpret them for Westerners. His major work was entitled *Essays in Zen Buddhism*. Some argue that his translations and interpretations went overboard in emphasizing the iconoclasm and spontaneity of Zen, in order to make it more palatable to Europeans. Nonetheless, his influence was pervasive during the first half of the twentieth century, and most Westerners who embraced Zen from the 1930s to the 1960s did so through Suzuki's books.

**Left** Roshi Harada (1870–1961) was one of the first masters to introduce Zen teaching to the West, making the teachings of both the Rinzai and Soto schools accessible to Westerners.

## Watts, Ginsberg, and "Beat" Zen

Suzuki's works were read eagerly by a 15-year-old British boy named Alan Watts (1916–1973), who even at such a tender age was obsessed with spiritual issues and growth. Finding his stern Anglican upbringing arid, rigid, and stultifying, Watts "sought refuge in Buddhism" and by his early twenties was editing *Buddhism in England*, the UK's first Buddhist magazine. Watts met Suzuki at the World Congress of Faiths in 1936 and, fascinated with Suzuki's endless *mondo* (Zen tales), started a lifelong friendship.

Watts began to publish his own interpretations of Zen, highlighting its liberating, iconoclastic aspects and de-emphasizing its relationship to Buddhism as a faith based on the practice of *zazen* (sitting). In his most famous book, *The Way of Zen*, read by generations of acolytes, he claims never to have found a single reference to this major aspect of Zen practice. Needless to say, when the first modern generation of Americans encountered Zen temples firsthand during the occupation of Japan in the late 1940s and early 1950s, they were astonished to find Zen monks sitting, chanting, lighting incense, and bowing to statues of Buddha. Suzuki and Watts had prepared them for something much more intellectualized and irreverent.

**Above** Many people seek connection to a higher power or something greater than themselves. This can be achieved in many ways. Zen Buddhism does not pretend to be the only way; only the most direct.

**Below** The counterculture of the late 1960s drew inspiration partially from Zen Buddhism. Into their spiritual blender they also tossed LSD and the Pill, producing a potent mix of sex, drugs, and rock 'n' roll whose allure survives today.

## "Repose beyond faith"

Meanwhile, on the American West Coast, especially in San Francisco, a new generation of postwar poets and seekers had discovered Buddhism, primarily through the works of Suzuki and Watts. One day a young man named Jack Kerouac opened a biography of the Buddha, purely by chance, and saw the phrase "repose beyond faith." Soon he was meditating and spreading the word about Buddhism and Zen to friends like the poet Allen Ginsberg, who eventually took Buddhist vows as an unofficial "teacher." Poet Gary Snyder, another member of the San Francisco "Beat" scene, ended up spending 12 years in Japan studying at a Buddhist monastery. J. D. Salinger, in his stories about the Glass family, helped to bring Buddhist and Zen ideas to an even wider audience, although at the cost of turning himself into a hermit, deeply wounded by the fanatic adulation that his works received.

Through books such as *On the Road* and *The Dharma Bums*, Kerouac reached a huge audience of disaffected American intelligentsia who found the world around them as colorless and meaningless as Watts had earlier in the London of the 1930s. They were attracted to the freedom that was offered by Zen; it gave them a spiritual basis for their nonconformity, and all too often became an excuse to eat and drink too much, pursue marital infidelity, and wander around the countryside, all in the name of satori. Watts, alarmed by the "do what feels good" atmosphere that he himself had helped to start, attempted to ground Zen in a spiritual soil by writing articles such as "Beat Zen," "Square Zen," and "Zen" (for the 1958 edition of the *Chicago Review*), in which he attempted to distance himself from his acolytes—although by then the damage had been done.

## The 1960s: the "True Birth" of Zen in the West

The Beat generation was a significant force in American culture of the 1950s, but in terms of sheer numbers its successors, the "baby boomers," exercised a much greater cultural pull. With their coming of age in the 1960s came the "counterculture," which was an umbrella for every kind of teenage rebellion. Much has been written about that; one of its sidelines, however, was that as many young people drifted to San Francisco for free music and free love, they found the San Francisco Zen Center, which had been founded in 1962 by Shunryu Suzuki (no relation to Daisetz), and were attracted by its philosophy and its promise of spiritual peace. The center began to attract a growing number of people to its services and *sesshin*, or retreats.

Shunryu Suzuki had arrived in America in 1959, and wrote one of the best introductory Zen books still in print, *Zen Mind, Beginner's Mind*. Also on the West Coast during this period was Roshi Yasutani, who visited the country in 1962 and arrived permanently in 1965, at the age of 80, to expound the dharma in the West.

With several "genuine" Zen masters now conveniently on United States soil, Americans no longer had to make the journey to Japan for their Zen experience. And for the first time Americans such as Philip Kapleau began writing about Zen more comprehensively, with specific instructions concerning the way in which to perform zazen. *The Three Pillars of Zen*, Philip Kapleau's most famous book, became a bible (of sorts) to a generation of "hippies" who had dropped out of mainstream culture and were looking for alternative methods of spiritual connection.

San Francisco continued to be the epicenter for Zen practitioners, but as acolytes moved away and fanned out over the vast continent, Zen centers sprang up everywhere, from upstate New York to Texas, from Toronto to Anchorage. Zen masters from Korea, Vietnam, and China recognized opportunities to found *sangha*, or Buddhist communities, and came over to America to establish their own temples and schools.

However, the very success of the Zen centers contributed to growing pains of one kind or another. There was a large cultural divide between the Asian roshi and their Caucasian students, resulting in miscommunication, misinterpretation, and misunderstanding. Some roshi seemed a little overeager to confirm successors in the interests of continuing their dynasties. The new breed of American-born Zen master was not able to command the same respect as his Asian predecessors. The behavior of some of the roshi (both Asian and Caucasian) did not conform to Western mores—or to Buddhist ideals either; rumors of financial and personal impropriety began to surface. However, despite these problems, Zen grew beyond its hitherto "fringe" status, with a few fusty scholars, and became a living, breathing, working community in the West.

**Below** Many Westerners have made pilgrimages to Japan, Thailand, and other countries of the Far East in search of "pure" Zen Buddhism "uncorrupted" by Western influences—ignoring the fact that Zen itself is a melange of Indian, Chinese, and Japanese thought, practiced differently in every country.

**Right** Zen Buddhism is not a cult; you will not find bald, robed Zen novices handing out flowers and pamphlets at airports and in other public places.

## The decline of Zen in Japan

Ironically, as interest in Zen peaked in the West, it began to wane in its host countries. Japan embraced Western consumer culture and its trappings of success, much as earlier generations of British and Americans had abandoned their Judeo-Christian roots to worship at the Temple of Mammon.

Left Buddhism has spread worldwide, with the most rapid growth in Western countries. It is also undergoing a renaissance in the East.

## The present day

According to Martin Baumann of the University of Hannover, there were roughly five million Buddhists living in the Western industrialized countries in the mid-1990s, out of a total population there of about 800 million; of these, about one million were European or American. There are now 500 Buddhist centers in America alone, and more than 1,000 in Europe and North America combined. In Britain, the number of Buddhist organizations tripled between 1975 and 1991. While Baumann's figures do not differentiate between the many Buddhist schools, the figures still illustrate the growth of Buddhism as a whole in the West.

As more and more people born into the Judeo-Christian faiths make connections to Buddhism, writers and scholars from these traditions have attempted to analyze the attraction that Buddhism has for Jews and Christians. Rabbis and priests, such as Zalman Schachter and Hugo Enomiya-Lasalle,

### The effect of the Web

With the growth of the Internet, information about Buddhism and Zen now circles the globe hundreds of times a week. Web sites offering daily koans and advice on Zen practice abound. Some sites for your perusal are listed on pages 140–141.

have even tried to construct hybrids that are rooted in their home faiths but utilize Buddhist practice, as an invigorating and refreshing "tonic" to draw in new adherents.

Of course, millions of people in the East and Far East are Buddhists by birth, although Buddhism has never been the religion of the majority of Asians. Due to its nature, Buddhism is not a strongly proselytizing faith, and its adherents have been subjected to suppression and persecution by Islam, Confucianism, and Hinduism—not to mention colonial Europeans. After falling into decay during the eighteenth and nineteenth centuries, Buddhism is making a comeback of sorts in the East, even in the land of its birth.

Ironically, it was the discoveries of shrines and inscriptions by Western archeologists in the eighteenth and nineteenth centuries that sparked a renewed interest in Buddhism in India. These discoveries—as well as the publication of an English-Pali dictionary in 1875—excited the interest of Indians who had forgotten the great heritage of their Buddhist past. With the ending of British rule in 1949, many sacred Buddhist relics were returned to India as part of its decolonialization. In 1956 India marked the 2,500th anniversary of the birth of the Buddha with numerous celebrations as well as an international conference.

As for Zen in Japan, most Japanese Zen Buddhists belong to so-called "New Religions," or sects, which are not descended from Zen but have in fact grown up around various personalities and masters, who are attributed with divine or magical powers. They appeal to people from rural areas, and are essentially lay organizations with no priestly structure. The most prominent of these sects are the Rissho Kosei Kai and the Soka Gakkai.

**Above** As Buddhism reveres no godhead in the Judeo-Christian sense, many elements of the philosophy are not necessarily incompatible with other religions.

# The Origins of Zen
## 10 Questions & Answers

**Q** Is Zen a religion, a philosophy, or a cult?

**A** Zen is a school of Buddhism, which is both a philosophy and a religion, but it also incorporates Daoism, which is a philosophy. It is a cult neither in practice nor in belief, since it does not demand absolute obedience; nor does it practice "brainwashing" techniques on its members. For more discussion on this, see the beginning of Chapter 2.

**Q** Is there any historical proof that the Buddha actually existed?

**A** There are many stories about the life of the historical Buddha. His birthday and death-day are part of the Buddhist calendar. There seems to be about as much proof of his existence as there is of most other major spiritual fathers—that is to say, minimal.

**Q** Did the Buddha have other disciples besides Maha-kashyapa?

**A** Traditionally, there were 10 major disciples in the Buddha's lifetime. Zen does not claim to be the only legitimate interpretation of the Buddha's teachings—only the most direct one.

**Q** I've heard that there are two main branches of Buddhism. What are they?

**A** Buddhism does indeed have two main branches. One is the Theravada branch, which believes that Enlightenment is personal; it arose in southern India. The other is the Mahayana branch, which believes that external forces can induce Enlightenment; it arose in northern India. Zen belongs to the Mahayana branch. There is, however, a third branch of Buddhism unique to the Himalayan region.

**Q** To which school of Buddhism does the Dalai Lama belong?

**A** There is in fact a third branch of Buddhism that is peculiar to the Himalayan region, called the Vajrayana branch, which incorporates Tantric philosophy. All three branches of Buddhism are respected by followers of the Lamaist school.

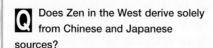

**Q** Does Zen in the West derive solely from Chinese and Japanese sources?

**A** After being brought from India, Chan Buddhism (as it was then called) flourished in China and spread throughout South East Asia. Thus many Zen practitioners today draw on sources from Laos, Thailand, Tibet, Vietnam, and Korea (among other countries).

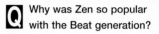

**Q** Why was Zen so popular with the Beat generation?

**A** Zen, as interpreted by Suzuki and Watts, seemed to offer a way out of the gray conformity of postwar America. It was swift and violent, crude and muscular. It offered a *raison d'être* to a fringe culture critical of formalism. It seemed adaptable to jazz, painting, and poetry—three of the most popular expressions of Beat culture.

**Q** Was Zen historically the most popular religion in Japan?

**A** No. That honor belongs to Shinto, Japan's native religion. Zen was favored by a select few: warriors, painters, and ascetics.

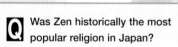

**Q** Why was San Francisco the entry point of Zen in North America?

**A** Many Chinese and Japanese workers were imported to the United States in order to build the Transcontinental Railroad in the 1850s. Their port of entry was usually San Francisco, which thus became the first major center for Asian culture in North America.

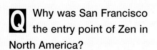

**Q** Is Zen the most popular form of Buddhism today?

**A** Far from it. Zen adherents form a relatively small minority of Buddhists worldwide. Since Zen Buddhists do not actively proselytize, this will probably not change in the future. Amidist Buddhism, which is less philosophical and more devotional, remains the most popular school in the Far East.

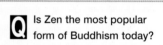

# 2 The Main Precepts of Zen

Zen claims to be the best, but not the only, vehicle for the transmission of the Buddha's insight. One of the appealing things about Zen Buddhists is that they tend not to be dogmatic or doctrinaire. They acknowledge other paths to spiritual awakening, and encourage seekers to try them all.

## Zen as a school of Buddhism

Many religions place heavy emphasis on the memorization of laws and precepts; often this aspect alone is considered "spiritual observance." Unlike such religions, Zen places the highest emphasis on experience as spiritual observance. This does not mean that serious Zen practice scorns ritual—far from it—but that ritual is constantly referred to as a vehicle for focusing the mind and body, never as a mode of worship in itself. One Zen master, Kubota Juin, has said that "Zen practice begins with belief and ends in actual experience."

So far "Buddha" has referred to Siddhartha Gautama. But the word *buddha* in Sanskrit simply means "one who is alive to the fundamental meaning of existence." The Buddha was just one of the many buddhas who have existed, both before and after the historical Buddha. Thus, in other contexts, a buddha can be anyone who has achieved Awakening. An object's buddha-nature is its "true" nature.

**Left** *Dharmacakra* (the Wheel of the Buddhist Law) represents the cycle of reincarnation. Siddhartha's first sermon is referred to as the "turning of the Wheel of the Law," that is, setting the wheel in motion. In early Buddhist aniconic art, Siddhartha is represented by either the bodhi tree under which he attained Enlightenment or by the wheel.

## Attachment and suffering

Buddhism is based on Three Precepts:

*All things in life—objects, thoughts, and feelings—are ephemeral; they are born, live, and then die according to unpredictable patterns.

*All life is inherently painful, because people base their lives around desires, and thus the root of suffering; our unceasing longing for wealth, status, children, power—and even life itself—is the root of our misery in this world.

*The third precept is harder to put into words and can only be perceived directly by experience. It states that there is a fundamental illusion behind all reality (like Descartes' character "Evil Genius," in his discussion on "What is reality?"); everything springs out of a common Great Void and returns to it in an endless cycle. But this Void is not a nihilistic black hole, which is how many outsiders understand the term "Void." Rather, it is vibrant and positive.

## The wheel of death and rebirth: samsara and nirvana

According to the Buddha, all beings die and are born again, as part of this endless cycle of entering and leaving the Void. Like waves on the ocean they rise up, temporarily (and falsely) believing in their existence as independent beings, and then fall back, returning to the great ocean of consciousness. This cycle of death and rebirth is called *samsara* and is inherently full of pain and suffering.

The Buddha's Awakening revealed that the cycle of samsara could be transcended; his experience taught him that the endless cycle of birth and death could be broken with

**Above** The wheel of life held by the demon-protector Mahakala, who mocks the desire that ties us to samsara. The outer ring represents causation; the inner areas reveal karmic consequences, paradise, and torments—metaphors for moving up and down the scale of reincarnation.

true awareness and understanding of the Three Precepts. No longer constrained by attachment to ephemera, beings were able to attain *nirvana*—the state of having escaped suffering by exiting the cycle of life and death—returning to their essential buddha-nature.

## The Four Vows, the 10 Abstentions, and the Three Treasures

All Buddhists recite these Four Vows every day:

*All beings, without number, I vow to liberate.*

*Endless blind passions, I vow to uproot.*

*Levels of understanding, I vow to penetrate.*

*The Great Way of Buddha, I vow to attain.*

Being a Buddhist thus means devoting yourself to following in the Buddha's footsteps. The 10 Abstentions are the actions that Buddhists are supposed to avoid. They are:

- The taking of life
- Theft
- Lack of chastity
- Lying
- Selling or buying liquor
- Speaking ill of others
- Praising oneself
- Giving spiritual or material aid grudgingly
- Anger
- Disparaging Buddhist doctrine.

The 10 Abstentions form one of the Three Treasures of Buddhism. The other two Treasures are: practicing goodness to avoid evil and striving toward the liberation of every living being (that is, helping others attain buddhahood). Oddly, this does not generally translate into aggressive evangelism among Buddhists, and Zen Buddhists in particular (in the tradition of Bodhidharma) tend to discourage spiritual seekers. Newcomers are encouraged to try Buddhism and judge it on the basis of their own experiences.

**Above** Different schools of Buddhism have slightly different sets of precepts, but they all adhere to the Three Treasures: cease evil deeds; practice goodness; help others to attain buddhahood.

## Bodhisattvas

Every once in a while a being, out of compassion, defers its exit from samsara in order to help others attain nirvana. This is akin to a potential Olympic gold medalist hanging back and helping the other contenders so that all are able to cross the finish line together. Beings such as this are known as *bodhisattvas*. These beings symbolize empathy, compassion, wisdom, and the ultimate in selflessness (as Westerners understand it). Those who have heard the term through songs by Steely Dan (from *Countdown to Ecstasy*) and/or the Beastie Boys (from *Ill Communication*) are forgiven if they thought that it meant something else.

**Left** Monks often seek secluded places to meditate—not only to commune better with nature, but also to enhance their "sitting power." Isolation helps focus; it can also be a hindrance if the sitter loses contact with daily life.

### Karma

Although cause and effect are considered to be illusory, their mechanism lives on in Buddhism under the concept of *karma*. In a simplistic sense, karma is a tally of the good and bad deeds that a being accumulates—not just over a single lifespan, but through an eternity of rebirths. As each being dies and returns to the Great Void, its "karma tally" determines how it will be reborn. Buddhists imagine a Great Chain of Being, from the lowliest protozoan all the way to the most perfectly evolved buddha. Each being thus rises and falls in a kind of spiritual stock market.

## Zen on its own

Zen shares the basic doctrines and tenets of Buddhism. While it believes that all beings can escape samsara and achieve nirvana, it differs in its beliefs as to how Awakening can be achieved. Other strands of Buddhist thought have (according to Zen teachings) more or less departed from the original idea of a perfect Transmission without words, forms, or distinctions. It seems to be human nature to surround mystical ideas with ritual, canon, and dogma. Zen Buddhism seems to have succeeded remarkably well in keeping these at bay by using shock tactics and humor. One famous Zen saying translates as "What is Buddha? Buddha is toilet paper." In other words, where other Buddhist sects have tended to put the Buddha on a pedestal, Zen—by means of juxtaposition—reminds us that what is sacred is profane and vice versa.

There is another Zen saying that *"The finger pointing at the Moon is not the Moon,"* Yet another states, *"If someone comes to you screaming, 'I am starving,' do you hand him a menu?"* The point these sayings are trying to illuminate is that truth can only be perceived directly. Studying it, or talking about it, or praying for it—all of these are often confused with the real thing. People get caught up in memorizing laws and precepts, and in arguing about minor theological points, and in the process they forget their original purpose: to achieve Awakening. That is why the Buddha often avoided words in his teaching; words are part of the curtain of illusion separating us from the truth.

**Below** Living organisms such as trees and even leaves are often used to explain Buddhist spiritual growth and development in that they renew and die off seasonally, yet return in a similar state each time.

### The experiential nature of satori

 Satori is the Japanese word for Awakening (another term is *kensho*). Again and again Zen masters emphasize that satori cannot be learned—it can only be experienced. No one story, sutra, or koan encapsulates the truth; all these things can do is to catalyze a change in the state of mind of the student so that he or she achieves direct perception of the same Three Precepts that the Buddha apprehended beneath the bodhi tree.

The author Raymond Smullyan uses humor as a metaphor for Awakening. If you don't "get" a joke, no amount of intellectual analysis or study is going to make it funny for you—either you get it or you don't. People with no sense of humor can spend all their time aping the behavior of those who have it (we've all met people with fake laughs and predigested amusing anecdotes), but in the end there is no substitute for actually having a sense of humor.

More than many other religions, Zen does a good job of consistently reminding spiritual seekers (often rather jarringly) that its forms and rituals are mere aids in seeking Enlightenment. Dogen's saying *"When you see the Buddha on the road, kill him"* is one of the most extreme examples of this. Westerners—especially the Beat generation and those influenced by them—often interpret these stories out of context as an excuse to do as they please. The fact is that many Zen masters utter disparaging remarks about themselves, Zen practice, the sutras, and even the Buddha in order to make the point that attachment to sutras, or to Buddhism itself, is still attachment.

> " *The finger pointing at the Moon is not the Moon.* "
>
> ZEN SAYING

## The Oxherding Pictures

In Pali commentaries there is a statement that goes thus: "Just as a man would tie to a post a calf that should be tamed, even so here should one tie one's own mind tight to the object of mindfulness."

In Chinese Daoism the use of an ox or bull as a metaphor for wisdom was well known. This metaphor was frequently illustrated by a series of pictures in which a man sought and conquered an ox, whose skin gradually lightened from black to white, symbolizing the purifying of the mind. By the twelfth century C.E. a series of pictures representing the Zen experience first appeared, credited to Guoan Shiyuan, a Chinese Zen master. They have become the most popular metaphorical explanation of the experience of seeking and achieving satori. Many prominent Zen masters have published their own versions of the pictures, often drawn by hand and accompanied by annotations. On the next few pages you will see the pictures, Kuo-an's poems (translated by Nyogen Senzaki and Paul Reps), and our interpretation.

> " *Just as a man would tie to a post a calf that should be tamed, even so here should one tie one's own mind tight to the object of mindfulness.* "
>
> PALI STATEMENT

**LOOKING FOR THE OX**

*In the pasture of this world, I endlessly push aside the tall grasses
   in search of the bull.
Following unnamed rivers, lost upon the interpenetrating paths of
   distant mountains,
My strength failing and my vitality exhausted, I cannot find the bull.
I only hear the locusts chirping through the forest at night.*

The typical person looks everywhere for peace of mind, even though he or she doesn't have to search—wisdom is right in front of his or her nose! Instead, they get caught up in all sorts of diversions.

Looking for the Ox.

Noticing the Footsteps.

NOTICING THE FOOTSTEPS

*Along the riverbank under the trees, I discover footsteps!*

*Even under the fragrant grass I see his prints.*

*Deep in remote mountains they are found.*

*These traces no more can be hidden than one's nose,*

*looking heavenward.*

The seeker hears about Zen, learns a bit about it, does some reading. He's still caught up in the dualities of existence, but has a glimpse of something beyond. It's exciting, but seems far away.

---

Catching Sight.

CATCHING SIGHT

*I hear the song of the nightingale.*

*The sun is warm, the wind is mild, willows are green along the shore,*

*Here no bull can hide!*

*What artist can draw that massive head, those majestic horns?*

After a bit of Zen practice, the seeker experiences a microscopic Awakening, a vision of some underlying pattern connecting him to the existence around him. There it is!

---

Getting hold of the Ox.

GETTING HOLD OF THE OX

*I seize him with a terrific struggle.*

*His great will and power are inexhaustible.*

*He charges to the high plateau far above the cloud-mists,*

*Or in an impenetrable ravine he stands.*

After more intense Zen practice, the seeker realizes the immensity of his task. Calming and purifying the mind are a lot harder than they sound!

### TAMING THE OX

*The whip and rope are necessary,*

*Else he might stray off down some dusty road.*

*Being well trained, he becomes naturally gentle.*

*Then, unfettered, he obeys his master.*

After much struggle, the seeker realizes that his thoughts and emotions are useful tools, as long as he rules them, and not vice versa.

Taming the Ox.

### RIDING HOME

*Mounting the bull, slowly I return homeward.*

*The voice of my flute intones through*

   *the evening.*

*Measuring with hand beats the pulsating harmony,*

   *I direct the endless rhythm.*

*Whoever hears this melody will join me.*

The seeker's understanding deepens, and becomes even more rooted in reality. Serene, unflappable, he is able to handle most temptations and distractions. Look how happy he is!

Riding Home.

### OX VANISHED, HERDSMAN REMAINING

*Astride the bull, I reach home.*

*I am serene. The bull too can rest.*

*The dawn has come. In blissful repose,*

*Within my thatched dwelling I have abandoned the whip and rope.*

Eventually the struggle recedes into the memory. In fact, it loses all meaning as the seeker really begins to understand that he and the ox were never separated to begin with. For those who truly understand, practice is no longer necessary.

Ox Vanished,
Herdsman Remaining.

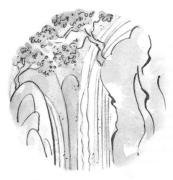

Ox and Herdsman Vanished.

Returning to the Source.

Entering the Marketplace.

### OX AND HERDSMAN VANISHED

*Whip, rope, person, and bull—all merge in No-Thing.*

*This heaven is so vast no message can stain it.*

*How may a snowflake exist in a raging fire?*

*Here are the footprints of the patriarchs.*

This is the blissful "oceanic" feeling described by Sigmund Freud, the transcendence of all ideas and things. All duality has vanished into the pure Void. The series used to end here, because what could come after perfect transcendence? However, Kuo-an felt that this did not in fact tell the whole story.

### RETURNING TO THE SOURCE

*Too many steps have been taken returning to the root and the source.*

*Better to have been blind and deaf from the beginning!*

*Dwelling in one's true abode, unconcerned with that without—*

*The river flows tranquilly on and the flowers are red.*

Too many people get stuck in the bliss of the previous step, never to emerge. The true Zen master returns to the real world, realizing that all is as it should be—not an illusion after all, but a manifestation of the Void.

### ENTERING THE MARKETPLACE

*Barefooted and naked of breast, I mingle with the people of the world.*

*My clothes are ragged and dust laden, and I am ever blissful.*

*I use no magic to extend my life;*

*Now, before me, the dead trees become alive.*

The final step is to return to daily life, like Joseph Campbell's *Hero With a Thousand Faces*, changed by the experience but ready to face the world. He is unremarkable to other people—but not the same man who went seeking the ox.

The Oxherding Pictures provide a convenient set of milestones for Zen practitioners. If you meet another Zen believer, you can ask about the status of their struggle with the ox and be pretty confident of getting a meaningful reply. Some people get stuck at one stage or another, or even abandon the path altogether. But everyone can place themselves somewhere on the journey.

## Zen schools

There are many schools under the Zen umbrella, each of which draws its authority from a particular Zen master. The two main schools practiced in Japan are the Rinzai and Soto schools. They constitute the majority of Zen practitioners in Japan and, by transmission, in the West.

**RINZAI** The Rinzai school was founded by Eisai, based on the teachings of Linji, a late-ninth-century Chinese Chan master. Its philosophy is that satori can only be achieved by actively penetrating the constraints of mind and logic. To this end, the Rinzai school uses koans to consume the mind and induce a state more conducive to satori. Koans (*see* Chapter 3) comprise riddles, stories, poems, and questions that are paradoxical or nonsensical. In Rinzai temples, practitioners face the wall during services to provide the least possible distraction.

After a period of decline, Rinzai was resuscitated by Hakuin Ekaku (1686–1769), who systematically reorganized the sect and its writings. He also invented new koans, including the famous "What is the sound of one hand clapping?" He was also a master artist, equally comfortable in calligraphy, painting, and sculpture.

**SOTO** The Soto school was introduced by Dogen in 1227. Dogen was orphaned at the age of eight, and undoubtedly this contributed to his introverted nature. Even as a child, he was obsessed by the question *"Why strive after perfection if we are already perfect?"* He achieved satori under Eisai, and spent more than 10 years at Eisai's monastery at Mount Hiei. Still spiritually unfulfilled, despite his progress, he wandered from place to place, even venturing on the hazardous journey to China, where he finally achieved total enlightenment. In his major work, the *Shobogenzo*, written over a 25-year span,

**Below** The Kondo or main hall of a Japanese Buddhist temple, where lectures, sutra readings, and important meetings are held, functions as the heart of every temple. The daily activities of monks will include cleaning duties, maintenance, and other domestic chores in addition to study and meditation.

Dogen addresses all matters concerning Zen practice, from toiletry to time and space. He seems to anticipate Albert Einstein with his discussion of "being-time."

In Soto temples, Zen practitioners face each other during services. Within Japan itself, adherents of the Soto school far outnumber those of the Rinzai school. Soto practice is so austere that it seems to abjure its followers from seeking Enlightenment because to do so is to attach oneself to the concept of "Enlightenment."

The Zen master Nyogen Senzaki once compared the Soto and Rinzai schools as follows: "Among Zen students it is said that *'Rinzai's teaching is like the frost of a late autumn, making one shiver, while the teaching of Soto is like a spring breeze, which caresses the flower, helping it to bloom.'*"

### Hybrids

Until the late nineteenth century Rinzai and Soto were considered quite separate schools of Zen. With the dawn of the twentieth century, Roshi Harada (*see* Chapter 1) believed that a synthesis of the two schools was not only possible but desirable. Harada realized that Rinzai and Soto had much to offer each other in terms of practice. Furthermore, masters from both schools borrowed liberally from each other's texts and traditions. And, in principle, attachment to one or the other was against the spirit of Zen in the first place. Harada and his disciple Roshi Yasutani spearheaded the bringing of Zen to America. Thus many North Americans who practice Zen draw from both schools; roshi use koans and shikan-taza, according to the needs and aspirations of the individual seeker.

**Above** The white lotus is symbolic of bodhi, the Buddha nature, due to its purity and perfection. Its eight petals correspond to the eightfold path.

# The Main Precepts of Zen
## 10 Questions & Answers

**Q** Is the Buddha a god (or God)?

**A** Buddhists consider the historical Buddha to be a human being who happened to be highly evolved in a spiritual sense; not a god with supernatural powers.

**Q** Why does Buddhism seek annihilation of the soul?

**A** This question betrays a misunderstanding of the use of the word "Void" in Buddhism. The Great Void is not a "black hole" that swallows everything; it is Existence itself. Souls are not annihilated by the Void; they are created by it and return to it.

**Q** What is an object's buddha-nature?

**A** Think of this as the object's essential essence—what makes it especially itself. The concept is vaguely Platonic—the "ideal" chair contained somewhere in the chair.

**Q** Do I have to take vows or chant precepts in order to practice Zen?

**A** The vows and precepts are there as moral guidelines. The idea is that, as your Zen practice deepens, you will naturally begin to follow the precepts; the corollary is that it is impossible to practice Zen seriously without following the precepts or taking vows.

**Q** Is karma the same thing as sin?

**A** The answer depends on your definition of sin, which in turn depends on your upbringing. Suffice to say that karma carries no innate sense of judgment; it is a self-correcting mechanism by which beings rise and fall toward Enlightenment. Karma is very contextual, and much depends on the state of mind of the person who is committing the act, whereas sin often connotes absolute right and wrong.

**Q** Are samsara and nirvana the same as heaven and hell?

**A** No, although it is natural to think so. At one level of understanding, according to some Zen masters, samara and nirvana are no different from the world you already live in! It is only your experience of your surroundings that translates into samsara for some, nirvana for others.

**Q** If I accumulate enough good karma in this life, will I achieve nirvana?

**A** Not necessarily—it all depends on the karma that you have earned over previous lifetimes.

**Q** What are the basic texts of Zen?

**A** The answer depends on the school that you follow. The *Diamond Sutra*, the *Kegon Sutra*, and the *Heart Sutra* (or *Shingyo*) are all revered texts derived from Sanskrit. Other books, such as the *Shobogenzo*, the *Mumonkan*, and the *Hekigan-roku*, are collections of koans and commentaries from the Japanese.

**Q** Does it matter which school I choose?

**A** All schools provide possible paths to Enlightenment. It is probably best to find the school that best suits your personality; this necessarily entails some "shopping around." Seeking a school is an honored tradition, as long as it does not become an excuse for dilettantism.

**Q** If I already have a buddha-nature, then why am I not already enlightened in the way that Buddha was?

**A** Now that would really make a good koan!

# 3 The Basics of Zen: Zazen

You could be excused if, even after reading three chapters of this book, you are still not sure what Zen practice actually comprises. What is it that all these monks, patriarchs, and students do in order to achieve satori? Do they pray? Sacrifice? Whip themselves into a frenzy? The answer is pretty anticlimactic.

## The idea: just sit!

When it comes down to it, Zen practice is all about sitting—and that's pretty much all there is to it! When you strip away all the trappings from Zen (the history, the precepts, and the aesthetics), all that is left is zazen. Literally, this means "sitting Zen." Many Zen masters maintain this is all there is to Zen; everything else is unnecessary, and even distracts the seeker from attaining satori.

Zazen is not meditation, in that someone doing zazen is not visualizing or chanting. Many traditions, both Eastern (even Buddhism itself) and Western, use meditation of some kind. Zen masters have nothing against chanting or visualizing; they simply tend to feel that they are barriers between the sitter and direct knowledge of the world. The brain is already cluttered with sensory stimuli and memories; why stir up the waters with more pictures and song?

**Left** One of the fundamentals of Zen practice, *zazen* means "sitting zen." The idea is that this sitting enables the practitioner to clear the mind and become "passive observers of their own thought processes."

The image of muddy water is common in Zen writings about the mind. Zazen is an attempt to still those waters and allow the mud to settle to the bottom, leaving cool, clear water behind. Once the mind is settled and "put in its place," all kinds of insight are possible.

How is this stilling of the mind achieved? The basic idea is that we "just sit," watching our thoughts rise and fall, and attaching ourselves to none of them. We become passive observers of our own thought processes, trying to "bite our own teeth," as the Zen masters say. Naturally, there is a kind of paradox in monitoring your own mind; you can end up in infinite regress: *I am watching my mind watch my mind watching my mind …"* and so on. But that paradoxical state of mind is exactly the one that Zen attempts to foster.

In this chapter you will learn all about several methods practiced by various Zen schools, from simple ones that can be followed when you are on your own at home to more complex practice that should only be attempted under the tutelage of an accredited Zen master.

**Right** Stone and rock represent the endless cycle that affects even the hardest substances.

> " *From the pine tree*
> *Learn of the pine tree*
> *And the bamboo*
> *Of the bamboo.* "

BASHO, ZEN POET
1644–1694 C.E.

## Getting ready

Before even beginning to sit, you should start to get into a more focused state of mind. In more formal environments this is done by lighting incense sticks, bowing, and reciting some texts. For many, it simply involves removing all distractions (including telephones, stereos, and pagers) and slowly settling into a sitting posture.

## Posture

The ideal posture for zazen is the full lotus position, with both knees touching the ground. To achieve this, you need a high cushion to sit on. Traditional sitting cushions are called zafu and are filled with goose down; failing that, a sufficiently high pile of pillows will do. Variations of the full lotus position include the half-lotus, quarter-lotus, and the Burmese position. In the half-lotus position, the left foot is placed over the right thigh and the right foot is under the left thigh, with both knees touching the mat. In the quarter-lotus position, the left foot rests on the calf of the right leg, with both knees resting on the mat. In the Burmese position, the legs aren't crossed at all; the feet rest one in front of the other on the mat (it doesn't matter which), and the knees rest on the mat. It is also possible to use a "kneeling chair" (on which you kneel rather than sit).

There was a time in the East when sitting in the lotus position was a common part of existence—falling into it was as easy for most people as falling off a log. Today it is rather more uncommon, and Westerners often find having to sit all pretzeled up quite painful, and soon tire of it. That is why many people do zazen sitting on a chair, with their feet flat on the ground and their spine not resting against the back of the chair.

The important points are that your spine is straight, your ears are in line with your shoulders and the tip of your nose with your navel. Your knees should be in line with each other, and your stomach and buttocks should stick out slightly. You should not be looking straight ahead, but slightly downward, so that your chin is drawn in and the back of your neck is slightly stretched. Your eyes should be open, but not wide open. The tip of your tongue should rest against the back of your front teeth. Now you are ready!

**Below** There are all sorts of mystical reasons why the lotus position is the optimal one for zazen. One is that it brings the spiritual centers of the body into alignment; another that by immobilizing the body, it becomes easier to immobilize the mind.

Some people prostrate themselves before and after sitting, with their palms upward and outward. This can be done whether or not you have a statue of the Buddha in your zazen space—the point is not worship of a deity, but a gesture of thankfulness toward all things. You should gently settle into your sitting position, rocking back and forth slightly. Gradually come to a stop and begin your zazen in earnest.

## How long to sit

Beginners are usually advised to sit for short periods to prevent them from becoming discouraged and falling away from practice altogether. At first it may be a triumph for you to sit for five minutes at the lowest level of counting breaths. As you continue to practice you will find that you are able to sit for longer and longer periods. In Zen centers and temples, adherents sit for different lengths of time, but generally sessions last between about 30 and 45 minutes. Sitting for longer periods than this at a single stretch is thought to be counterproductive, as your focus slackens.

At temples and sesshin (Buddhist retreats), sitting periods are broken up with periods of *kinhin,* or "walking zazen." These are rounds of ritualized walking, sometimes accompanied by drumbeats, during which adherents remain focused but turn their attention to the act of placing one foot in front of another.

## When to sit

Zen centers and temples generally hold zazen sessions in the mornings and evenings, before and after work. In monasteries and sesshin, zazen sessions are held throughout the day, broken up by kinhin and meals.

If you are starting off on your own, it is best to sit every day—and at the same time every day. Make a schedule and stick to it. Sitting once in the.morning and once in the evening is recommended, although for many people this isn't possible. If you have a choice, the morning is better, because distractions are likely to be fewer. However, sitting in the evening is preferable to not sitting at all. Sitting after meals is discouraged, because digestion makes most people feel sleepy.

## Counting breaths

Roshi Yasutani, in his introductory lectures, got novices to begin by counting breaths. There are three levels of breath-counting, from easiest to hardest:

* Counting "one" with the first inhalation, "two" with the first exhalation, "three" with the second inhalation, "four" with the second exhalation—and so on, up to 10.

* Counting "one" with the first exhalation, "two" with the second—and so on, counting only exhalations, up to 10.

* Counting "one" with the first inhalation, "two" with the second inhalation—and so on, counting only inhalations, up to 10.

While counting breaths, the intention is not to stop thinking. Far from it! The intention is to let the mind wander where it will, but without attachment. Stray thoughts will enter, physical sensations will come and go; the challenge is to let such feelings flow over and through you. When you get caught up in some train of thought (and you will—often—when you first begin), don't reprove yourself. Gently bring yourself back to your breaths and begin again from one.

At first just getting to 10 once, without becoming distracted, will be very difficult. There is no point in trying to cheat yourself. Letting your mind sneak away to plan dinner or tomorrow's presentation defeats the purpose of zazen. Other typical distractions include:

* Getting lost in a haze of memories.

* Worrying about things on your "to do" list.

* Playing back over and over again an argument you had with your partner or boss.

* Worrying about your aching back/knees/buttocks.

* Wondering when zazen will be over.

**Above** During zazen practice, allow your mind to wander but detach yourself from any thought process.

**Left** A level of austerity can be found in all schools of Buddhism, harking back to the period in which Siddhartha joined the ascetics of the forest to find nirvana. In rejecting asceticism, however, he developed the "middle path" toward nirvana based on the music master's admonition, "if the string is too taut it will break, but if too loose it will not play."

## Shikan-taza

In the Soto school, counting breaths is soon supplanted by simply following the breath in and out of the nostrils, known as *shikan-taza*. Students are generally able to remain undistracted for long stretches of time; if they do get caught up in their thoughts, they gently return to following their breath.

Shikan-taza is considered one of the highest—and hardest—levels of zazen to maintain. The practitioner is not supported by visualizations, chanting, stories, or riddles; he or she simply sits with the attitude of a mountain or a tree, implacably and exquisitely surveying the world. Thoughts, feelings, even the yearning for satori—all these are left behind. In shikan-taza, the very act of zazen is the highest manifestation of one's buddha-nature. Nothing more is needed.

Some practitioners in the Soto school take this attitude even further, saying that since zazen is the best we can achieve, satori itself is undesirable, because it fosters attachment. This is a very austere philosophy, requiring a lot of faith on the part of its adherents; it is very difficult to sustain without the support of fellow-practitioners and a roshi.

### Ending your sitting

In Zen centers and temples it is the job of one of the congregation to mark the end of the zazen session by banging a gong or ringing a bell. Sitters slowly rock back and forth on their pillows, then gradually rise and begin kinhin, or simply walk off their cramps. Those practicing at home may have to settle for an egg-timer or radio alarm, although there are special "zazen alarm clocks," which go off in ever-increasing bell-like tones. However you mark the end of your zazen, do not immediately resume your hectic life. Give yourself a couple of minutes to slowly reemerge into daily life.

**Above** A peaceful monastery nestled beneath the arms of a mountain, a Zen ideal for the mountain representing Mount Sumeru and the power of nature versus the insignificance of the individual.

" biting one's own teeth "

KOAN MASTER

## Koans

In the Rinzai school, once the student has become accustomed to sitting practice, he or she is given a koan to occupy his or her time while sitting. The koan is not a mantra or a visualization—it is a method of exhausting and taming the conscious mind by forcing it back on itself: *"biting one's own teeth"* is the way some masters put it.

One of the most famous koans is one of the most basic, and is often given to beginners. It is the first koan in the *Mumonkan (The Gateless Barrier)*, one of the central texts in Rinzai Zen, which comprises a collection of 48 koans, each accompanied by a commentary and a short poem by Mumon.

Mumon was born in the twelfth century, toward the end of the Sung Dynasty. He studied at Manjuji Temple under Roshi Getsurin, a strict teacher who gave him the koan "Mu" to study (see below). After six years Mumon still had not solved it. He swore he would not sleep until he understood Mu, and whenever he felt sleepy he would go out into the corridor and bang his head against a post. One day, when the noon drum was struck, Mumon suddenly achieved satori and in celebration (as was often the custom) he composed the following verse:

*Out of a blue sky, the sun shining bright, a clap of thunder!*
*All the living things of the great earth open their eyes widely.*
*All the myriad things of nature make obeisance;*
*Mount Sumeru, off its base, is dancing.*

The next day, when he interviewed Roshi Getsurin, Mumon wanted to tell him about his experience, but Getsurin asked, "Where did you see the god? Where did you see the devil?"

Mumon said "Katsu!"—an exclamation that is halfway between "Ole!" and "Oh, hell!"—and Getsurin knew that Mumon had reached Enlightenment.

Here is the koan "Mu" in its entirety:

*A monk asked Joshu: "Does a dog have buddha-nature?"*

*Joshu retorted "Mu!" [That is, "No!"]*

Here are excerpts from Mumon's commentary:

*To realize this wondrous thing called Enlightenment, you must cut off all discriminating thoughts. If you cannot pass through the barrier and exhaust the arising of thoughts, you are like a ghost clinging to the trees and grass.*

*What then is this barrier set by the patriarchs? It is Mu, the one barrier of the supreme teaching. Ultimately, it is a barrier that is no barrier. One who has passed through it can not only see Joshu face to face, but can walk hand in hand with the whole line of patriarchs...*

*How marvelous! Who would not want to pass through this barrier? For this you must concentrate day and night, questioning yourself through every one of your 360 bones and 84,000 pores. Do not construe Mu as nothingness and do not conceive of it in terms of existence or nonexistence... Eventually you feel as if you had swallowed a red-hot iron ball that you cannot disgorge... When you have cast away all illusory thought and discrimination...you will be like a mute who has had a dream—but cannot talk about it...you will be able to slay the Buddha should you meet him and he attempt to obstruct you..."*

And here is Mumon's short poem that accompanied the commentary:

*A dog, have buddha-nature!*

*This is the presentation of the whole, the absolute imperative!*

*Once you begin to think "has" or "has not"*

*You are as good as dead.*

**Below** Forests appear as obstacles to the traveler, to light, and to open space, but the Enlightened individual passes through obstacles as easily as light penetrates a wall of trees.

## Solving "Joshu's Mu"

So what's all the fuss? Well, the problem is that, if all beings have buddha-natures (which they do, according to Buddhist thinking), then why did Joshu answer in the negative? That in turn begs the question of why the monk asked Joshu "in all seriousness." Didn't he know? Was the monk having a crisis of faith? Did Joshu think that a contradictory answer would jolt the monk into Enlightenment?

You may now get a sense of how a koan can bury its way under your skin, sending you back again and again to the beginning, each time without a complete answer. It is this frustration that Zen masters call "doubt"—that red-hot cannonball in your stomach that you carry around all day and cannot expel. There is a saying in Zen: *"Small doubt, small enlightenment; great doubt, great enlightenment."* There are people who attain satori relatively quickly and easily, but the effects quickly wear off, because their original effort was slight.

How do you know when you have solved the koan of "Joshu's Mu?" If you believe Mumon, you will know when you have solved it, because you will be able to see Joshu and all the patriarchs face to face. What this means is naturally unclear, but some have interpreted it to mean that everyone who achieves satori taps into the same "channel" and, at least for some moments, sees the universe exactly the way the Buddha and the patriarchs did.

**Below** Attacking a koan head first with logic is like staring at the sun in that it damages rather than helps. Yet sunlight illuminates from all sides.

Of course, for Zen Buddhists only a certified roshi can ascertain whether a student has truly "solved" "Joshu's Mu." This is usually done in a personal interview called a *dokusan*, which takes place during a sesshin. In the interview, the roshi tests the student with questions. Once satisfied that the student has indeed solved the koan, the roshi gives the student a new, more difficult koan. Over time, as the student solves more koans, he or she achieves deeper levels of satori; a monk living and studying in a monastery accumulates greater prestige. Since dokusan are private, the answers to koans are very secret. And a good thing, too—otherwise anyone could just memorize the answer, go in, and fake it!

Indeed, over the centuries books of koan "solutions" have circulated secretly among the monasteries so that ambitious students could rise through the hierarchy and even be certified as roshi themselves. In this way many Zen masters arose who had never actually experienced satori. Naturally this corruption caused the Rinzai school to lose much credibility. Today more effort is spent on ensuring "quality control" among Rinzai roshi and students. The important thing to realize is that there is rarely just one solution to a koan. To one who has attained satori, the very idea that a koan has even one solution at all is rather comical! Koans are meant to break the spirit of the rational mind; once solved, they can be forgotten.

**Above** If a monk living and working in a monastery has solved many koans, he or she is held in high regard.

" *Small doubt, small enlightenment; great doubt, great enlightenment.* "

ZEN SAYING

# The Basics of Zen: Zazen
## 10 Questions & Answers

**Q** What frame of mind should I be in when I sit?

**A** You should be calm, yet focused. Some Zen masters say that you should think of yourself as a tree or a mountain—implacable and indomitable.

**Q** I can't sit still for more than five minutes at a time! Am I a hopeless case?

**A** Not at all. There is no point in forcing yourself to sit for longer than you can manage. If you persist, you will find that you are gradually able to sit still for longer. One factor could be external distractions. Make a real effort to block off some time when you will not be disturbed.

**Q** How long should it take me to move through the various stages of counting breaths?

**A** That differs from person to person, and there is no set timescale. There is no use in being impatient. And it is quite possible to achieve satori from any stage of zazen, if the motivation and proper focus are present.

**Q** My legs always cramp up and/or fall asleep when I try to sit in the lotus position. What should I do?

**A** Some stretching of the legs and back before sitting will make zazen easier. If the problem persists, you can always shift to using a kneeling chair, or even a regular chair. Better to sit than not do zazen at all.

**Q** When I just sit, I have the most fantastic visions. What do these visions mean?

**A** These are very common and are called *makyo*. Even the Buddha had makyo. Zen masters make it very clear that makyo of any kind are imaginary products of the mind, and thus illusory. They mean nothing. Let them pass, as the Buddha did, and push on for satori!

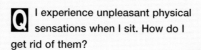

**Q** I experience unpleasant physical sensations when I sit. How do I get rid of them?

**A** Itchiness, bloatedness, nausea, burning, and other miscellaneous sensations are all distractions fomented by your mind in its attempts to break free. Don't let them distract you! You can use them to investigate the ephemeral nature of all thoughts and sensations.

**Q** When I sit I get drowsy. What can I do about this?

**A** You could try sitting in the morning rather than the evening. Temperature could also be a factor; open a window and get some air circulating. If you feel sleepy whenever you sit, that is simply your mind trying to evade your efforts to tame it (see the previous question).

**Q** I have "out-of-body experiences" when I sit. What should I do?

**A** These are another variation of makyo (see above). All of a sudden "you" will be seeing out through your belly, or your knees, or the back of your head. Again, allow these feelings to pass through and do not cling to them.

**Q** Can I work on koans alone?

**A** Most masters agree that this is unwise. Without the guidance of a roshi, you will never really know if you have solved them. The temptation to "cheat" can be quite strong. You might choose a koan that is too hard, get frustrated, and then give up entirely.

**Q** How long does it take to solve a koan?

**A** There is no ideal timescale. Some people struggle to solve just one koan in their whole lives; others seem to be able to whizz through them. It all depends on your motivation, focus, and frame of mind.

# 4 Zen at Home

As we saw in the last chapter, all you really need in order to "sit zazen" in your home are a few pillows (or a straight-backed chair) and a blank wall on which to focus. For some people, that is all that is necessary—or possible.

## Making your house a shrine

If you live in a small house or apartment with no room for a permanent Zen space, you may have to set up and take down your zazen pillows every day. This is not an onerous task, especially if you turn it into a mindful activity, a kind of warm-up and cooldown before and after your zazen session. If space allows, however, the enthusiastic practitioner could find an unused corner of their home in which to set up a permanent zazen area. Over time, this space can grow into a sort of shrine, depending on your level of involvement.

There are doctrinal issues involved here. On the one hand, Zen masters argue that there should be no artificial separation between zazen and the rest of life; this would be to make unnecessary distinctions. On the other hand, students of Zen seem to benefit from setting aside a space and a time to confront the mind and make it submit. Rituals are an important part of life, and Zen Buddhism is not averse to them as long as they are not confused with the attainment of Enlightenment (the finger pointing at the Moon, see page 28).

**Left** Sitting in a chair is sometimes the only way to perform zazen if you lack space. Your back should be straight, your hands gathered in your lap, and your eyes partially closed.

**Above** Even the smallest space can be converted into a shrine, with enough mindfulness. You can use a folding screen to create your own separate zazen space.

**Above** The fragrance of flowers can enhance zazen—but they should not be in your line of sight when sitting.

**Below** Your sitting space may include a shrine to the Buddha. It is important to understand you are not worshiping Buddha— merely walking in his footsteps and expressing gratitude for his teaching.

### Possible additions to your zazen space

靈感

- Incense cones or sticks
- Statue of the Buddha
- Fragrant flowers
- Hangings with sutras written in calligraphic script
- Other pieces of art that promote mindfulness.

**Above** Incense is another way to increase focus during zazen.

You might consider putting up a screen in order to separate your zazen space from the rest of your dwelling. This could be either a folding screen of light wood and paper, such as are found throughout Japanese buildings, or a more utilitarian Western version. The purpose of the screen is symbolic: it is temporary and incomplete, to remind you that, while zazen requires a brief absence from other daily routines, it is part of an integral whole.

## Lighting and accessories

Your zazen area should be well illuminated by natural daylight, but you should avoid direct sunlight beating down on you. If the area is near a window, you may by all means have it open while you do zazen. Many practitioners have achieved satori by listening to the incessant chirping of insects or beating of rain. If you live near a construction site or an all-hours club, you might experience a modern-day satori from the pounding of jackhammers or the drum'n'bass from next door!

Aside from your pillows, kneeling chair, or straight-backed chair, you may want to add various other accessories to your zazen space (*see box left*), with the purpose of helping to still the mind and promote a calm and focused attention. Your field of vision as you sit should be blank when you do zazen; if you find yourself overstimulated, then consider removing the distraction.

The more serious you become about your Zen practice, the more your zazen space may come to resemble an actual Zen temple. This is fine, if it is what you want. On the other hand, you may be content with just some pillows and a blank wall. It is completely up to you.

## Zazen with groups at home

Many Zen masters maintain that doing zazen in groups is helpful, because members can encourage each other and feed off each other's energy. If you happen to live far from a Zen temple or center, then the only way for you to experience this is to invite a group of like-minded Zen students over for a group zazen session (see also Chapter 10). Here are some thoughts about arranging your dwelling to accommodate a group.

You will need a large room with a great deal of floor space. The walls should be as blank as possible; you might have to put some paintings in storage. Ideally, the floor should be made of wood and uncovered, except for the areas immediately surrounding each person's sitting pillows, which should be covered with mats. You may want to ask people to bring along their own sitting pillows and/or chairs; alternatively, you could provide for your guests.

If the group is Rinzai, people will face the walls; if the group is Soto, they will face the center of the room. Depending on the time of day and the position of the windows, curtains may be open or closed so that the room is lit naturally, without direct sunlight shining into anyone's eyes. Fluorescent lighting should be avoided.

You will also need some kind of timer—preferably nothing too jarring. If you can get your hands on an hourglass, you can time your zazen without the intrusion of an alarm. More serious practitioners might sound a small gong at the beginning and end of zazen sessions.

**Below** You can do zazen in a group as well as on your own. If you there isn't a Zen center near you, you can arrange a group session at home with other Zen students.

It generally helps if one person leads the other Zen students in a zazen sitting—but this person need not be the most experienced student of the group. You may also want to rotate the leadership in order to give everyone the experience. At Zen centers and temples, the roshi or senior monk generally leads the sittings.

## Dealing with distractions

Aside from distractions such as pagers, telephones, and stereos, there are issues involved in sitting at home. Since the point of zazen is to calm the mind, it doesn't help if every time you start, your partner wants to talk or your youngster comes in asking for help with his drawings. So, if you work from home, the possible distractions multiply (*see* Chapter 5 for a discussion of the implications). If your partner is at a different stage of practice, or not interested in zazen, there are other issues to be addressed (*see* Chapter 7).

Family members must be cautioned about interrupting your zazen. If you have young children, you may have to be flexible over your sitting times, grabbing whatever opportunities you can while they nap. With older children, you may be able to explain what you are doing and why, and make them understand that you need to be alone and must not be disturbed.

### Sharing zazen with your children

You might wish to have your children join you in zazen. After all, you may have heard that children in the East join monasteries. It is possible for children to sit zazen (depending on their age), but it is probably unwise to encourage it. Forcing children to sit still works against their buddha-natures as energetic explorers. You do not want to spend your zazen sessions monitoring your child. Let them come to Zen in their own time, of their own volition.

## Applying Zen principles to interior design

Taking a step back, you can ask yourself how to integrate Zen principles into your dwelling in order to encourage mindfulness and attention in all things. In the popular imagination, the word "Zen" is often used to refer to spare, utilitarian surroundings. It is worth considering how much of this belief is true and where it originates.

Studying the terms that form the basis of Zen esthetics in Japan (*see box*), it is not hard to see how they derive from Zen principles. In Zen there is a sense of the world being constantly in a state of flux. Thus a high value is placed on objects and spaces that appear fragile, even (or especially) if they are actually quite durable.

Since Zen attempts to eliminate all dualities, it follows that there is a great desire to blur all distinctions between "natural" and "man-made" objects. Instead, the goal is to imitate nature in all its functionality and simplicity. Related to this is the idea of the "happy accident." Zen cherishes one-time-only events and values improvization. The love of symmetry that has been a basis of Western art since the time of the Greeks (if not before) is quite alien to Zen esthetics.

Finally, the concept of the Great Void translates into a love of open space, whether in art or interior design. Space is not considered empty or wasteful; it is thought to be "full"— refreshing and inspiring creativity.

### Common esthetic terms in Japanese Zen

- *Yugen*: giving a glimpse into the Unfathomable
- *Aware*: pathos; the joy and sorrow of living
- *Wabi*: blending with the elegance of the natural world
- *Sabi*: serenity; melancholy; loneliness
- *Ichi-go, ichi-e:* one encounter, one opportunity.

**Right** Leaves speak of the transitory nature of existence, exploding with color before they are gone.

Integrating Zen principles into your home generally involves:

- Organizing living areas to maximize their space
- Eliminating unnecessary clutter
- Choosing furnishings and decorations that embody Zen esthetic values
- Harmonizing elements of a room into a coherent whole.

These tasks work synergistically, in the sense that accomplishing one always involves thinking of the other three—which serves the Zen ideal of thinking holistically.

The proper use of space is essential in Zen interior design. You can use closets, shelves, and irregularly shaped nooks to avoid clutter. Furnishings that can be folded up and set against a wall or stored in a closet are also excellent ideas. You can accentuate the feeling of space by using pale colors for walls and wallpaper, along with natural materials such as wood, brick, and stone. Large windows or skylights allow in natural light and provide opportunities to commune with nature.

Jane Tidbury, in *Zen Style: Balance and Simplicity for Your Home*, advocates sorting your clutter into logical groupings and displaying them in new and interesting ways. For instance, a junk drawer full of paperclips, Post-it notes, and rubber bands could be reorganized into a set of glass jars with wide mouths. However, she cautions against overdoing this—the end result might be just as haphazard-looking as what you started out with.

Vinny Lee, author of *Zen Interiors*, suggests using color to echo natural elements—red for fire, blue for water—and recommends natural textures such as wood and stone, whose quality is amplified by such colors. Lee also recommends using fragrances and sounds to stimulate all the senses and encourage serenity.

**Above** Zen design encourages open spaces and lack of clutter. Note the extensive use of storage space and natural materials.

**Right** Well-arranged flowers mimic nature while implying mindfulness in their gathering.

## Zen versus consumer culture

The world of the Buddha and his contemporaries was agrarian. People farmed or raised cattle, or made handcrafted objects and implements for sale. They worked from dawn till dusk, but there were no schedules because there were no accurate time-pieces. Trade routes were extensive, but uncertain; voyagers were at the mercy of the elements and marauding bands. Life was hard—but, on the flip side, most people were solidly root-ed in the present. Because their lives were directly connected to the cycles of the climate and land, they understood the idea that all things happen in their own time. Since they were virtually powerless, they were more accepting of the turning of fortune's wheel. Because they were poor, with few prospects for improv-ing their lot, they had few ambitions to better themselves.

Today, many of us make our living from jobs that are based on capitalizing on our own and other people's desires. Advertising, fashion, marketing, fundraising, business, law—such professions are all about attachment to things and, most of all, money. We often spend entire days at work without seeing the sun or going outside. Nature can seem threatening, because it is one of the few things we cannot control. Because communication networks have become so extensive, we are less and less able to "get away from it all." Most of us obtain the necessities of life from supermarkets and pharma-cies; when this system breaks down (during a blackout or storm) we become almost helpless.

So is Zen Buddhism compatible with this kind of world? You could ask the same question of Judaism, Christianity, Islam, or any other faith. And yet many people consider themselves good Jews, Christians, Muslims, and so forth, and still manage to live and work in this world.

You can integrate Zen principles into your home life, without sacrificing the many good things that come from being part of an advanced technological economy, by following this advice:

Simplify your life by getting rid of needless clutter around the house. Reducing your attachment to "things" is always valuable, if done in moderation (not everyone is suited to the life of a wandering mendicant).

Reduce your bad karma and increase your good karma by making ethical choices about the use of your money. Credit unions and ethical investment funds are more common than ever before—and provide as good a service and return on your money (if not better) as the mainstream alternatives. Join a food cooperative or buy produce from local farmers' markets, instead of from supermarket chains. Get involved in your local community by volunteering at a youth drop-in center, literacy program, or senior citizens' home.

Cultivate a feeling of appreciation of your fellow beings. This will become easier as you deepen your zazen and get past the illusion that you are a separate, independent entity.

Above all, maintain a studied detachment from the fad-a-minute, instantly obsolete culture in which you live. That doesn't mean that you cannot participate in it. But you will find, if you sit zazen regularly, that your mind will begin to settle. Soon, the obsessions that used to haunt you (do I have the latest clothes/CDs/Java applets?) will begin to pale and you will realize that everything is ephemeral, and that trying to have it all is to have nothing.

Everyone makes choices between lifestyle and spiritual beliefs. Buddhism's strength lies in its experiential nature; it is completely up to you to decide how much of it you want to incorporate into your life.

**Left** Although Zen Buddhism emerged from a rural, agrarian society, its precepts can be practiced by anyone, including those who live in a technologically sophisticated urban society.

# Zen at Home
## 10 Questions & Answers

**Q** I've tried separating my zazen space, but everything looks more cluttered. What am I doing wrong?

**A** You could try different arrangements, but there's no point in putting up partitions if everything ends up looking more crowded. If your zazen works without barriers, so much the better.

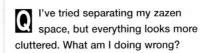

**Q** My partner/children are having a hard time leaving me alone for zazen. What should I do?

**A** Emphasize to them that you need your zazen time in order to be a better partner/mother. If they normally find you impatient and crabby, tell them that zazen will make you a more calm and balanced person. By appealing to their self-interest, you might get the time alone that you need.

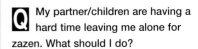

**Q** I don't have room for group zazen at my place—but I'd really like to organize something.

**A** If you are enthusiastic, but don't have the space, you could ask around and find out what facilities are available in your neighborhood. A local church, temple, or store might have some extra space that they would be willing to lend or rent cheaply.

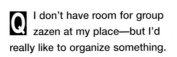

**Q** I've cleared away all my clutter, but everything seems barren and empty. Is it bad to go back to clutter?

**A** Some people need time to acclimatize to open spaces. If you are doing zazen, you will probably find yourself appreciating open spaces, the more you sit. But in the end, if it doesn't work for you, don't attach yourself to it.

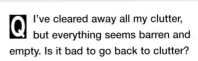

**Q** My house is all narrow hallways and small rooms. How can I achieve an open space?

**A** You could knock down some non-essential walls, or at least punch some holes through in order to provide more connecting areas between rooms.

**Q** Try as I might, I cannot get my place to look more harmonious. Is there anything I can do?

**A** You could call in a feng shui specialist. In the most extreme cases it is possible that you simply need to find a different space—one in which you can live in harmony.

**Q** What colors are best for decorating interiors according to Zen principles?

**A** Light, pastel colors are best for interior walls and surfaces, while natural earth tones are best for decorations and furniture.

**Q** I have wall-to-wall carpeting. Should I take it up?

**A** If you know you have wooden floors underneath, it may be best to lift the carpets and bring yourself into contact with the wood, although carpeting has some advantages. But there's no need to get attached to the idea that you have to replace all your floors.

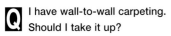

**Q** I am an obsessive collector. How can I be a good Zen student?

**A** Over time, if you practice zazen, you should find that your obsessive qualities recede. You can still enjoy a fine wine, a great book, or a funky CD, but you may find yourself satisfied to take the book out of the lending library, for instance, instead of buying it.

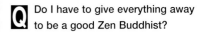

**Q** Do I have to give everything away to be a good Zen Buddhist?

**A** Not at all: the ascetic life is not for everyone. Buddhism does not demand that a vow of poverty be taken. It is possible to live a comfortable life without clinging to wealth and possessions. There are lots of ways to live a good life and at the same time generate positive karma.

# 5 Zen at Work

There is no escaping the fact that there seems to be a major divide between the beliefs of Zen Buddhism and the world in which most Westerners live and work. In this chapter you will learn how you can bring Zen into your working world. At one level, this refers to office design and layout; at another, deeper level, it is about integrating Zen principles into your day-to-day business activity.

## Zen versus corporate culture

Most of us work at jobs that the Buddha and the patriarchs would never have encountered, let alone understood. We work in the "new economy," an information-driven workplace that runs 24 hours a day, seven days a week. Many people have jobs whose very basis is aimed at increasing people's attachment to objects—in the process filling our minds with more and more "noise" in the name of commerce. Under the banner of "globalization," companies and their workers are pressured to be more productive

**Left** Even in the corporate world it is possible to apply Zen principles to your career and to the workplace.

## Removing distractions and freeing the mind

The aim is to make your work environment reflect a calm and still state of mind, uncluttered by distractions. The undistract-ed mind is more efficient, free to react quickly to all circum-stances. One author, Jeff Berner from California, favors preserv-ing as much roominess as possible by installing long, thin counters around the office for your current projects and the items you use all the time. In this way things have less of a tendency to pile up, which means that you don't waste so much time plowing through accumulated clutter.

**Right** If the Buddha were living today, would he have his own web site? Would he have his own cable channel? Would he have even attained Enlightenment?

and efficient. Resources (both human and physical) are stretched to their limits. The very basis of our economic system is a relentless Darwinism where only the strongest survive.

Obviously there are philosophical tensions between spiritual principles and the demands of the workplace—regardless of which spiritual discipline you follow. If you believe in the sacredness of all life, then you will have problems working in a slaughterhouse; if you believe in protecting the environment, then you are going to be uncomfortable writing advertisements for logging companies that pursue damaging foresting policies.

Many people reach a point in their lives when they can no longer reconcile their beliefs with their choice of career. That is why you hear of a bond trader quitting his lucrative job to start teaching literacy to inner-city children, or of couples deciding to live on a single income so that one partner can stay home to

look after the kids. Of course, many people make changes that are not quite so drastic. Others, such as Les Kaye, author of *Zen at Work*, manage to combine lives in the corporate world (in his case, IBM) with dedicated Zen practice (as a career monk and abbot of Kannon Do, the Zen meditation center in Mountain View, California).

Bringing Zen into the workplace may be as simple as rearranging the furniture or tearing down some walls. On another level, it may be about introducing or reemphasizing creativity and flexibility into workplace routines and tasks. At the deepest level, it may be about changing the underlying philosophy of your career path. This chapter begins with the esthetic issues. At a basic level, you can make changes in your work environment that reflect Zen esthetic principles such as yugen, wabi, and sabi (*see* Chapter 4).

## The Zen of working from home

Eliminating clutter is particularly important if you work from home, as more and more people do. There can be a tendency to take your work with you wherever you are in the house (even if you have set aside a room for "work"), leaving paper trails as you move from "work" room to living room to bathroom—talking all the while on your cellphone.

It is no good making a separate area for sitting zazen if it ends up being cluttered with stray faxes and printouts. Resolve to keep your workspace separate from your other spaces. This is particularly difficult if you live in a house built around lots of open spaces, such as a loft. In this case, you might consider putting up a partition or thin screen to demarcate your working area. You could also consider the use of bulletin boards, sticky boards, and whiteboards, so that you can lay out your designs and work on the walls, instead of taking up room space with tables and desks, which are magnets for bits of paper and other flotsam.

**Above** Zen is about transcending distinctions; it is also about keeping your life free of clutter. If you work at home, keep your workspace and zazen space separate; make a conscious effort to take an occasional break.

**Below** Large piles of paper are often a signal to reduce clutter. Create efficient storage space in your office in order to reduce time lost searching through mountains of files and correspondence.

## The workplace sanctuary

It is worth emphasizing that work-related objects and storage should not overlap with recreation or relaxation space. In the interest of "saving space," some offices shove photocopiers and filing cabinets into the staffroom, intruding upon what should be a sanctuary. Employees need areas where they can temporarily break away from work and recharge their energies. The overall harmony of the work environment should be preserved by making room for every office function.

# The Zen of office design

Zen principles can also be applied to office design. Eliminating clutter and encouraging "flow" can be done in any space, using feng shui and/or simple common sense. The emphasis on roominess does not necessarily imply a "wall-less office"—although many businesses today are set up along such lines. In fact, a totally open work area can be harmful, because it does not allow for the private space that people need. Of course for some businesses this is exactly the point: they want to minimize their employees' privacy out of the fear that giving workers a place to "hide" will lead to more shirking. However, any workplace that has reached this level of suspicion has problems that require a great deal more than repainting the walls and building some shelves.

If you are in charge of renovating the office and want to do so along Zen lines, then by all means open up the workspaces, reduce clutter, knock down some walls, put in some windows and skylights—all of these are positive moves. But you could also allow people to design their own workspaces (within limits). There is no point in clinging to the idea of open workspaces if the office as a whole cannot work that way.

The fact is that some people like clutter—or at least seem to work better amid it. We all know people with workspaces that, to the untrained eye, might resemble Utah Beach after D-Day—but ask them for a file from 18 months ago, or a three-hole-punch, and they will have it on your desk within five minutes. Again, attachment to a particular office design in the face of uncooperative coworkers will hardly generate good feelings (and thus positive karma) around the office.

**Left** Zen encourages graceful flow and movement. A well-designed office incorporates both open space and private space.

## Zen principles on a grand scale

As an example of the way in which the office environment can be reworked to promote Zen principles, Nortel Networks, a worldwide telecommunications company located just north of Toronto, faced the challenge of redesigning its global headquarters. It took its old factory, once used to make telephone equipment, and transformed it into a fully wired community. The offices are color-coded "neighbors," which are clearly laid out and easy to navigate. But the designers have not forgotten about the employees' need for rest and sanctuary: there are basketball and volleyball courts, seven indoor parks, and even a Zen garden. They have also thought about the practical requirements of the company's workers, providing a full-service bank branch, fitness centers, dry-cleaning services, a travel agency, and a variety of cafés and restaurants within the building, so that employees do not have to rush all over the city to get various mundane tasks done. This does not of course mean that the business is not a commercial enterprise, but it cannot help but foster a calmer, more focused environment.

## Applying Zen principles to your career

The dedicated Zen practitioner uses Zen as more than just a set of esthetic principles. As we saw in Chapter 2, remaining true to the way of the Buddha and the patriarchs means looking at your life in a fundamentally different way. This section discusses the ethical implications of bringing Zen into the workplace, and discusses some typical workplace issues from a Zen perspective.

The Four Vows of Buddhism are very much a personal commitment to achieving Enlightenment— not just for yourself, but for all beings. The main precepts provide an ethical foundation, which can (and indeed should) be brought into the workplace.

Obviously if your career involves the continuous violation of one or more of the precepts, then you are in a position to accumulate a great deal of bad karma.

Even if this violation is not directly due to your specific actions, the bad karma is still yours. Naturally some professions are more vulnerable to breaking the precepts than others; looking down the list, politicians seem liable to break several a day.

In all seriousness, the more you integrate Zen Buddhist beliefs into your day-to-day life, the more difficult it may be for you to conform to certain expectations of your employer. Resolving these conflicts may be as simple as rearranging your schedule or as difficult as changing careers entirely.

## Cultivating detachment and focus

One way in which you can integrate Zen practice into your job is to focus on a single task at a time. These days there is a lot of pressure on employees to "multitask"—and many people get quite good at it. The problem is that when you multitask, you scatter your energies. Resolve to stop doing more than one thing at a time. We all know how hard it is to get something done properly if we are distracted. This does not mean that you have to finish one task completely before beginning another one; simply that when you are working on something, you should bring your undivided attention to it. If you are filing, file; if you are answering calls, then answer calls.

**Opposite left** In the rush to amass power, wealth, and status, it is easy to lose touch with the precepts; however, the more you practice, the more grounded you will be in the dharma, and the less attached you will be to samsara.

**Below** There are many informative web sites about Zen Buddhism (*see pages 140–141*); there are, however, no substitutes for zazen and following the precepts.

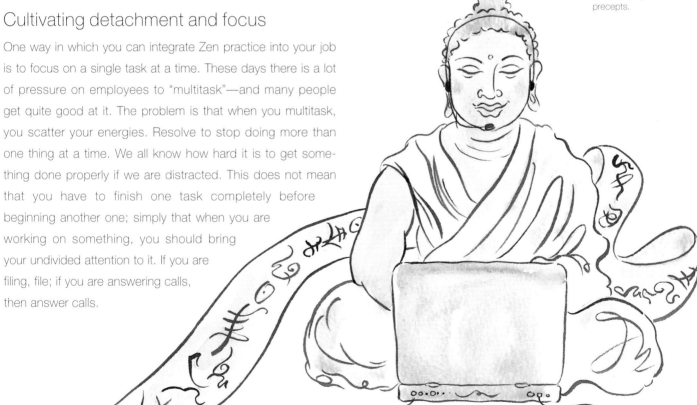

> *Flow with whatever may happen and let your mind be free: Stay centered by accepting whatever you are doing. This is the ultimate.*
>
> ZHUANGZI
> CHINESE PHILOSOPHER
> 369–286 B.C.E.

It isn't easy to cultivate nonattachment at work. Details are always dancing around us, begging for our attention; office procedures often seem petty and irrelevant; coworkers can rub us the wrong way, or—more seriously—may be actively working to frustrate us and thwart our goals. Dealing with these kinds of daily irritants can be difficult. One Zen amateur from Staten Island, known only as "Tim," has summarized on the Web some lessons he has learned from Zen via the martial arts (*see* Chapter 8):

Flexibility over strength. Be like water; flow around obstacles (including people) that impose themselves in your way. Naked assertions of power are brittle.

Control your emotions, or they will control you. The angry person will defeat him- or herself in battle as well as in life.

Recognize the inherent harmony of everyday life. Seek balance in your life between work and home, work and family, work and yourself.

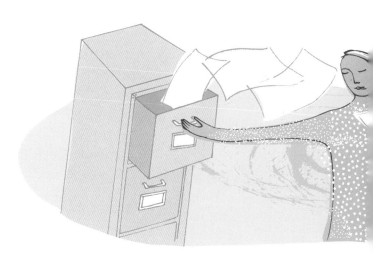

Recognize the priceless irreplaceability of the present moment. Living for the moment does not mean, however, that you shouldn't plan for the future or learn from the past.

Empty your cup, and fill it with today's lessons. You are getting feedback every moment of every day—use it.

Focus on process, not product. Keeping your goals in mind is important, but focusing totally on them usually distracts you from working effectively at your present task. If you attend to your present work properly, you will meet your goals.

Train yourself to respond unconsciously, not intellectually. Simple things, including most "people skills," are most effective when they spring, unforced, from your true nature. Who do you think is more effective: someone who is genuinely friendly and helpful or someone who is acting in this way because "it's their job?"

Fear is shadow, not substance. Most of our fears are about the future, which hasn't happened yet and isn't real. Fear drains energy from the present moment—energy that you can use to extricate yourself from your current predicament.

In order to outdo your opponent at his game, improve your own. The best way in which to win is not by pulling your opponent down, but by pulling yourself up. Of course some opponents can be pulled down by the sheer weight of their own imperfections—in which case all you need to do is simply tip them over.

Allow yourself pauses—the rest that refreshes. Without the pause, all you have is noise. Make time to clear your mind, because only a clear mind can act, and react, effectively.

**Left** Work can be a prison. Using the precepts of Zen Buddhism, you can liberate yourself from this prison, freeing yourself from the suffering that comes from clinging to unhealthy thoughts and emotions.

## Bushido: the code of the samurai

Of course there are other ways of integrating Zen into your working life. Some people have embraced the philosophy of the Japanese warrior class, or samurai, known as bushido.

Samurai is simply a term denoting the position of a retainer to a lord. Like the medieval knights of Europe, samurai were expected to bear arms in support of their feudal masters in times of conflict and to act as police in times of peace. The main symbols of their status were the privileges of having surnames and wearing two swords. Traditionally, samurai were paid in the currency of rice (coin being too base to handle) and served only for the honor of fighting and dying in the service of their hereditary masters. In reality, however, samurai could expect fiefs, estates, arms, and horses in return for good service. The poetic representation of the samurai had always been the *sakura*, or cherry blossom, which blooms for only a very brief time in the spring and dies without growing old, in a cascade of beauty.

## The way of the warrior

During the Tokugawa period (1603–1868) the image of the samurai—embodied by the way of the warrior, bushido—drew samurai and laymen to study the martial arts, strategy, and dueling. Death in battle, avenging a murdered or dishonored master, and committing suicide to preserve one's honor were glorified in literature, theater, and art, such as in the books *The Revenge of the Soga Brothers*, *The Loyal 47 Ronin* (masterless retainers), and the tales of the greatest swordsman Miyamoto Musashi. Bushido also lives on in the martial arts world (*see* Chapter 8).

> " *It goes without saying that as soon as one cherishes the thought of winning the contest or displaying one's skill in technique, swordmanship is doomed.* "
>
> TAKANO SHIGEYOSHI

## 10 sayings in the bushido tradition

Here are 10 sayings from writers in the bushido tradition that have interesting analogies in the business world:

"One finds life through conquering the fear of death within one's mind. Empty the mind of all forms of attachment, make a go-for-broke charge, and conquer the opponent with one decisive slash." Togo Shigekata

"An effective stance is to be attached neither to the opponent's sword nor to one's own sword." Yagyu Toshiyoshi

"The undisturbed mind is like a calm body of water reflecting the brilliance of the moon. Empty the mind and you will realize the undisturbed mind." Yagyu Jubei

"To be swayed neither by the opponent nor by his sword is the essence of swordsmanship." Miyamoto Musashi

"Conquer the self and you will conquer the opponent." Takuan Soho

"The mind unmoved by external distraction produces physical mobility." Yagyu Renyasai

"The hands manipulate the sword, the mind manipulates the hands. Cultivate the mind and do not be deceived by tricks, feints, and schemes. They are the properties of a magician, not of the samurai." Saito Yakuro

"Mental bearing (calmness), not skill, is the sign of a matured samurai. A samurai therefore should neither be pompous nor arrogant." Tsukahara Bokuden

"Conquering evil, not the opponent, is the essence of swordsmanship." Yagyu Munenori

"An unpolished crystal does not shine; an undisciplined samurai does not have brilliance. A samurai therefore should cultivate his mind." Anonymous

## 10 principles of Zen behavior
(adapted from Carol Orsborn, *How Would Confucius Ask For a Raise?*)

1. Balance and harmony in all things
2. All things are born, live, and die
3. You are imperfect and still learning
4. Lead by example
5. Know your place
6. Let your goodness shine through
7. Persevere
8. Come to terms with restrictions
9. Simplicity
10. Keep an open mind and a watchful eye.

**Below** The Edo period (1608–1867) brought relative peace to Japan. Without battles and strife, the samurai lost much of their purpose, regaining their martial spirit through literature, theater, martial arts, and dueling.

# Zen at Work
## 10 Questions & Answers

**Q** So how would the Buddha ask for a raise?

**A** Author Carol Orsborn suggests that he would work as hard as possible at his job until his bosses realized that he deserved a raise. Alternatively, he would set up a meeting with them for evaluation and goal-setting.

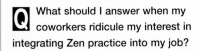

**Q** How can I find time to sit zazen at work?

**A** The simple answer is to close your office door, turn down the ringer on your phone, and let it be known that you are not to be disturbed. Even five minutes of such peace can be refreshing. Your commitment to clearing your schedule is the main thing.

**Q** I find it really hard to relax at work—my stress levels are way too high. What do I do?

**A** Something has to give. You are riding an out-of-control horse, and something is propelling you forward beyond all reasonable bounds. You need to sit and find out what that is. Give yourself permission to let go and accept what comes.

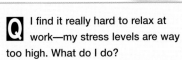

**Q** What should I answer when my coworkers ridicule my interest in integrating Zen practice into my job?

**A** That's their prerogative, and there is no point in proselytizing. The best thing that you can do is push on and prove, by example, that it "works" for you.

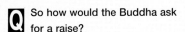
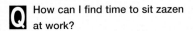

**Q** Is it okay to break off in the middle of zazen if I'm expecting an important call and the phone rings?

**A** No: if you are expecting a call, don't start to sit. Even better, try to make clear to people that you are unavailable from 10.00 to 10.15 (or whatever) every morning.

**Q** I enjoy my job, but don't think it has much potential for doing good. Should I change jobs?

**A** If you are unhappy in your present job, by all means consider a change. But it is possible to do good outside your regular job. If your work is karmically "neutral," but pays the bills, maybe that is all it's supposed to be.

**Q** I have a job that is karmically good, but doesn't pay much. Is it wrong to want a better-paying job?

**A** Of course not! You can't control your thoughts. The question is how you act on them. Keep the long-term karmic costs in mind—but remember that doing good grudgingly violates the precepts.

**Q** My boss has asked me to do something I feel is karmically wrong. I could be fired. What should I do?

**A** Breaking the precepts for the sake of work will harm you and others. Allow yourself to ruminate on the worst-case scenario; it could be that being fired would (in the long run) be the best thing that ever happened to you. Ultimately, it is your call.

**Q** I've been laid off and feel desperate. Can I take the next job that comes along, even if it's karmically tainted?

**A** You must weigh the long-term karmic costs and benefits. So much depends on your individual circumstances. Beware of being sucked into a "temporary" situation that becomes permanent.

**Q** I've given it all up for a simple, spiritual life—but now what?

**A** Were you expecting a medal? Satori? It sounds as if you used spirituality as an excuse to drop out of the rat race. Now you need to sit with your restlessness until you can stand it no longer—then something will happen to show you the way.

# 6 Zen Gardens

What is a "Zen garden?" There is no recipe for building a Zen garden in this chapter, any more than there is a recipe for Enlightenment in any part of the book. This is partially due to the fact that the concept of a "Zen garden" seems to be more a Western categorization than an Eastern concept.

## Zen and gardens

This chapter offers a discussion of how a "Zen garden" might differ from your current backyard arrangement, and what constitute the elements of a garden for Zen practice, through descriptions of some of the most famous Zen gardens and styles. As the box opposite suggests, what you decide on, what you create (or opt to leave out) will in the end be far less important than how you actually view your garden.

One explanation for the Zen association with gardens might be the fact that the legends of Bodhidharma (and, by connection, the early development of Zen practice and teaching) are all set out of doors: he meditated before a cliff wall for so long that his legs grew useless (hence the Daruma round-bottomed toy); he crossed the Yang-zi River on a reed; his first pupil got Bodhidharma's attention by throwing his own severed arm at him at the mouth of a cave. Nothing about Bodhidharma seems to have taken place inside a building, and this spirit has pervaded Zen thinking ever since.

**Below** Bonsai (dwarf trees) and scholar stones are two ways to bring a garden indoors. Alone they become art works in themselves, or can be matched to form vistas.

Although Zen influence has been strongest on Japanese culture, we should not assume that Zen does not play a part in the cultures of Korea, Vietnam, China, and other countries. In these countries, however, the influence has not been as all-pervasive as Shamanism, Daoism, Confucianism, and other Buddhist schools. With the backing of political power that Zen received during the past millennium in Japan—in the form of the Kamakura shogunate's patronage of early Zen temples and patriarchs, the Ashikaga shogunate's support of the *Nō* theater, Zen architecture and garden design, the relationship between the great tea-ceremony masters and the warlords of the Civil War era and Edo period—Japanese visual and performing arts, design, philosophy, and literature have all been imbued with Zen sensibility, to the point where they cannot be separated. In Chapters 6, 8, and 9 of this book, in particular, the focus has therefore purposely been placed on the influence of Zen on Japanese cultural phenomena.

**Left** In Buddhist iconography hand gestures (mudra) impart their own language. The raised right hand in *abhayamudra* indicates "coming in peace," the left hand pointing downward in *bhumisparsamudra* represents Sakyamuni calling the Earth to witness His Enlightenment.

## Making a "Zen garden"

Go out and buy 100 yards of white gravel, seven large boulders with weathered patina, and build yourself a meditation hall from which to view your handiwork. Spend a life's savings, work for five years to get it constructed, let it set for 300 years, and you will have one-hundredth of what you need for a "Zen" garden. Sit down, look at it properly, and it is complete.

## Back to nature

In most people's imagination a typical Zen garden is a clear expanse of raked gravel with a few well-placed rocks. Although it is a good example of one type of Zen garden, this image represents the style and esthetic of all Zen gardens no better than Beethoven represents all music. Shrubs, trees, flowers, grasses, ponds, moss, buildings, and other outdoor structures all play a role in different gardens. What separates a garden— or, more precisely, a "Zen garden"—from the general land-scaping of a temple's or monastery's grounds is an enclosure: whether real (as in the case of a walled area) or suggested (as in the case of a directed view). In either case, the garden is set aside as an area of focus, to be viewed from a vantage point rather than enjoyed from within. Although it may seem as though, in creating and viewing such a garden, a barrier has been created separating the individual from nature, in practice the garden and the viewer can become even closer—even though they are physically apart.

## The contemplation of nature

Just as Siddhartha reached Enlightenment below a bodhi tree, and Bodhidharma sat in a cave, so a small portion of the natural world is brought into Zen religious practice for more than decorative purposes. In many ways, this connection to the outdoors is also a result of Chinese influence on Zen and the ideal of the scholar recluse, which developed particularly in the Song period and pervades much of Chinese art from the twelfth century onward. Having fulfilled his duties serving the government as a bureaucratic official, the "gentleman" had as his goal retirement from public life to a country retreat among pine and bamboo groves in the mountains, to write poetry, play music, and contemplate the beauty of nature. The painting and literature of China, Korea, and Japan of the "literati" tradition clearly demonstrate this obsession with contemplating nature, much as early nineteenth-century Europeans were mad about all things "pastoral."

Even for those who never left the cities, their surroundings re-created the atmosphere they sought, if only in the form of a single view from a library window. Scenery was imported to their estates and mansions through gardens carefully designed to afford a variety of vistas within a limited space, and they were able to re-create a semblance of mountain scenery through the positioning of ponds and waterways, rockeries, artificial mountains, trees, and shrubs, which blocked views from certain angles. They controlled the way in which gardens were seen by means of paths and viewing places, framing the scenery with pierced walls, doorways, and pavilions.

In Japan, the Zen priest Muso Soseki (1275–1351) was one of the first to begin adapting existing gardens to match Song-style landscape painting, through the generosity of his patron, the shogun Ashikaga Takauji. Even famous Japanese painting masters, such as Sesshu and Kobori Enshu (1579–1647, and also a tea master), put their talents to the design of gardens. Such gardens recall the scenery of the "literati" genre of painting, in which perspective moves vertically—that is, those things that are higher in the visual plane are understood to be further away. Elements within the scene may also be separated using "cloud perspective," allowing a line of mist to symbolize movement further back into the plane of view. Garden designers used water, gravel, moss, and grass as a means of re-creating these forms of perspective.

Thus, from one vantage point tall trees might recall narrow, looming mountains over a river; from another position along the path, the same trees might become the mountains in the background of a wider lake view.

In both Japan and southern China a large number of the finest of these gardens, which once adjoined palaces and estates, have survived—often as bequests to temples and monasteries, which built halls and lodges around particularly good views, bringing their gardens of choice into courtyards and walled areas. It became standard that part of the "abbot's quarters" would always be a formal garden. In Japan prior to the seventeenth century gardens for contemplative purposes were designed or modified to provide stimuli that created both tension and tranquility: a smooth expanse broken by a rough boulder; an area of white interrupted by black; straight lines interspersed with wavy; a smooth cone abruptly cut off near its peak. Later gardens involved trees and shrubbery in a more integral manner, partially due to Zen sects such as Obaku, which tended to return to the esthetic of the more natural, softer Chinese tradition.

## The power of suggestion

Perhaps the single element that links all classic Zen gardens is the fact that the viewer is not meant to stand or sit and view the garden from within; rather, the view is usually appreciated from a path, a building, or a window. Adjoining halls might open visually onto the garden from walkways or walls of sliding doors, but rarely is there access to the garden. This could be regarded as the mind's recess from zazen, for apart from its decorative elements, a well-designed garden can be viewed as a visual

**Above** The moon-viewing lantern is a common site in both Zen and tea gardens. Bridges in many gardens at times lead nowhere or only to a further viewing place, but not much further.

**Below** Rounded rock shapes can add form to even the smallest bonsai arrangement, evoking waves and hills like the shrubbery of the garden opposite.

koan. The shapes and forms suggest something other than they are—an alternative reality hinted at by shape and form, but only a vague representation. If formal European gardens can be termed "literal" (there is no mistaking a topiary bush in the shape of a swan for something else, and a geometric maze or form is just that), then Zen gardens can be termed "suggestive." The forms of rocks, trees, water, and other elements and their combinations—either by design or by accident—are more than purely decorative in that they evoke images such as animals, scenery, religious images, and mythical beasts (rather like the childhood pastime of watching clouds). Just as the reality of Enlightenment exists all around us in the Zen view of the world, and we have but to recognize this to reach satori, so the reality of the true form of a tree or a raked-sand ocean is something that, when recognized, brings the practitioner closer to understanding. The viewer—though physically separated from the view—is actually within the garden as part of the continuity of Enlightenment. The realization of what the garden elements are, what they represent, and the reality of the surroundings mirrors the realization of the Buddha changing from Prince Siddhartha to the Tathagatha (He Who Has Traveled Forward and Returned—that is, the Buddha) under the bodhi tree.

**Above** Worn pebbles from a riverbank automatically bring to mind images of water and tranquility, waves and coolness.

**Right** Carefully groomed bushes and manicured moss fields are the pride of Japanese gardeners. Before winter, amazing coats and covers constructed of rope, straw, and bamboo are erected to protect less hardy details from the elements.

## Garden reality

Zen practitioners in Asia, although they may have gardens surrounding their homes, do not necessarily have contemplative Zen gardens, because they have some access to the gardens and grounds of temples and monasteries. In Japan, at least, it is common for a weekend outing to mix sightseeing with zazen and garden contemplation if you happen to be in Kyoto, Kamakura, or any other famous historical center. Such oases are not available to many in the West, leading those on the path to create their own "Zen gardens," whether this is the corner of an apartment balcony or involves a complete landscaping of the backyard.

Perhaps the easiest way to decide and choose which form of garden works for you and your surroundings is to describe some of the more famous gardens of Japan. These generalizations will enable you to visualize the different elements and possibilities: like a walking tour of the gardens, but with nontraditional commentary.

### Establishing the parameters

Scale and expense are of no consideration in creating your Zen enterprise, because your ability to use the garden is of paramount importance. A potted tree or houseplant can suffice to set an image and create an atmosphere for you, where a backyard sand mound might fail, if all you can envisage is the waste of a month's salary. Visit some garden centers, a few historical gardens, and consider the various possibilities before settling on a plan.

**Below** In this garden the rock grouping is framed by the wall, shrubbery, and sand expanse. When viewed correctly, the shrubbery takes the place of sails on the rock boat.

## The Rock Island: Ryoanji, Kyoto

This is perhaps the style that the term "Zen garden" evokes in most people's imagination. Within a sea of raked white gravel, the size of a tennis court and carefully reworked every day, a number of ancient-looking rocks are set—seemingly at random—none much larger than half a yard in height and diameter. Over time, a fine green moss has grown to ring each of the rocks. Three sides of the garden

**Below** The tendency toward wild and natural surroundings is found in few Zen gardens, and then only seen from certain angles.

are walled to eye level, widening the expanse of white in the view. The fourth side is the roofed side walkway of the temple hall, made of weathered planks of cryptomeria cedar that look as though they have been in place longer than the walls and stones. This view is said to evoke a mother tiger and her cubs in the snow, islands in the sea, the heads of horses as they ford a river, the tops of trees or mountains above the clouds, tree stumps…

## The Moss Forest: Saihoji and Kinkakuji, Kyoto

A carpet of moss is left to spread here over the exposed roots and undulations of the ground around old trees. If the moss is of a certain type, or if viewed from a proper distance, it can begin to look like tiny trees across a forest landscape, the roots and rises in the ground appearing as ranges of hills; with a few fallen leaves it becomes like the surface of a river in fall, or fine velvet. In the case of Saihoji, the moss garden is walled; at Kinkakuji it covers a cliffside.

## The Forest Mountain: Kenchoji, Kamakura

From the back of the 400-year-old hall of this quiet temple can be seen a low hill covered in a rich variety of bushes and low, round rocks. The trees overhead start at the far side and appear more as background, like the joins in a folding screen. The mix of textures and colors is clear, but subtle, for the shapes of bushes are differentiated between flowering and nonflowering in spring, leaf and needle in summer, and changing and evergreen in the fall.

## Mount Fuji: Ginkakuji, Kyoto

This single element is very dramatic and perhaps the most overt example of all the famous gardens of Kyoto. Raked sand is piled into a cone to approximately the height of a person, ending with a wide, flattened top. Smaller cones of sand (at times with pointed tops) are seen in other garden examples, erupting out of an expanse of flat raked gravel in some cases.

## The Dragon's Back: Kinkakuji, Kyoto, and MOA Museum Gardens, Atami

The courtyard of an L-shaped cottage across from the Temple of the Golden Pavilion is dominated by a gnarled pine, which is said to be related to the pines at Kamakura grown from the seeds brought from China with the first Zen teachers. This tree has been helped to survive for centuries and has been allowed or trained to grow in defiance of the laws of gravity. Its main branches stretch far longer than its height, supported by timber frames at intervals, like the supports of a train bridge across a chasm. This form can also be seen in many small bonsai that are trained in a similar manner to spread horizontally from a stout, stubby trunk; and in some larger gardens is re-created with a series of bushes, shaped into connected humps that trail into the distance or surround a large open area, as if coiling in sleep.

**Above right** At Ginkakuji in Kyoto, a carefully raked cone, with a flattened top representing Mount Fuji, creates a dramatic effect.

**Right** Very overt imagery is often a late Edo period statement in Zen gardens, as is seen in this nautical tree grouping. Pines and cedars are pruned and their roots cut to stunt or guide growth, just as for bonsai trees indoors.

## West Lake: Daisenin and Konji-in, Kyoto

Surrounding a small body of water and commanding three sides of a raked gravel area, low-rising hills are covered in a mix of short trees, bushes, and rocks to create a mountain scene reminiscent of Chinese landscape painting. Shugaku-in Imperial Villa and Saihoji, Kyoto, extend this along a continuing view of river or pond into the distance, copying hand-scroll paintings such as "Mountains and Streams Without End." Upright stones set with lower, wide boulders can create the impression of the enchanting scenery along the Li River in Guilin, where one passes "Praying to the Bodhisattva Mountain," "Great Apple," and "Descending Bat's Cliff," the inspiration for the oddly shaped mountains seen in many Chinese paintings.

## Lonely Pavilion: Sanzen-in and Shisen-do, Kyoto

A close growth of bushes conceals all but the upper section of a lantern, rising like the roofs of a pagoda above the trees, or a small flat rock under a tree simulates a mountain hut. This style is particularly adaptable to smaller gardens and bonsai arrangements, so that the focus is brought in, but should never be blatantly suggested with tiny ceramic houses and figures, as is done in some southern Chinese examples.

**Below** This elegant, but unobtrusive, Japanese stone lantern lends a focus to the scene and adds mystique and spirituality to the gardens.

## The Ocean: Nanzenji and Konji-in, Kyoto

The effect of a great expanse of raked white sand or solid green grass is best seen from a seated position, and from the interior of a hall, so that the peripheral view of the sides is controlled. The open space thus appears endless and the horizon interrupted only by the enclosure of the garden wall itself, as if the view continues well past. The feeling of open water is further emphasized at Nanzenji by the raking of the sand in long strokes, receding from the hall into the distance, with the center line flanked by undulating lines like a pattern of waves.

Most temples require daily raking of the sand gardens, a laborious practice and perhaps a form of meditation in itself. The pattern is rarely altered, rather repeated in the same manner each time, as devised originally by the garden's architect. As with calligraphy, a well-groomed sand expanse makes the activity of reproducing the pattern seem casual and effortless.

**Above** Open space is an important feature in Zen gardens. In this garden the wide expanse takes on the appearance of a tranquil sea or lake. It can be viewed from the interior of the hall, making it a perfect site for contemplation.

**Right** Are they small islands off the coast of a faraway shore, boulders against which the incoming waves crash and break up, or a church and a gas station in the middle of the prairies?

## A thousand pines

Many Zen gardens tend to minimize the use of flowering plants and shrubs. This is not because of dislike or prohibition, but more to emphasize the viewing of the garden as a whole rather than focusing on any one element. On the other hand, there are those gardens that use flowers and color in profusion and in doing so the emphasis on any single flower, bush, or shrub is diminished.

More often in a Zen garden, differentiation of shape and tone is achieved by placing a variety of contrasting textures together: for example, wild moss abutting carefully raked gravel; a slim conifer situated beside a broad-leafed tree; trees and shrubs whose leaves change color with different rapidity arranged together. Rather than emphasize the beauty of a single flower, the garden uses color as another shade with which the scene is painted.

**Below** Groupings of tall cedars evoke the feeling of a bamboo forest, but on a larger scale, and with greater permanence and light.

### Sincerity

There are endless possibilities for creating Zen gardens, both indoor and outdoor: ferns in front of a wooden fence; a spider plant cascading down the corner created by the side of a bookshelf and a wall; a garden hedge that trails off into the distance. In the end, whatever you create will serve, as long as you put some effort into the planning and what you plan reflects both you and your surroundings. The teachings of the tea master Sen Rikyu (1521–1591) discuss such sincerity in gardens on a visit that he made with his son to the gardens of another tea master in Kyoto.

By the path, Sen Rikyu's son praised a very weathered and moss-covered gate, remarking that it was the type of thing one might find on a secluded mountain path. The master agreed that it probably came from just such a location, and that the owner had obviously gone to great expense to bring it to his garden, where a gate of new wood would not have seemed out of place or any less expressive.

Just as a tropical garden in a cool climate will seem forced, so in the end overdone artifice will seem contrived, while a well-planned and fitting garden will succeed, even if it differs from the examples discussed in this chapter.

# Zen Gardens
## 10 Questions & Answers

**Q** Does a Zen garden have to be rocks and sand—and bare?

**A** The garden of rocks and raked gravel represents only one of many styles of Zen garden: the most austere, and therefore the least like a garden in the Western sense. For this reason it sticks in many people's minds. The ultimate expression, and most famous example of this type, is probably that at Ryoanji in Kyoto.

**Q** Am I limited by the seasons and the weather?

**A** Not at all. If planned with care, gardens can be just as beautiful and poignant covered in snow as they are in a tropical setting.

**Q** Doesn't all the expense and fuss of making a Zen garden go against the simplicity of Zen practice?

**A** Sincerity also plays a role in the development of a garden, ensuring that you do not go beyond your means. In many cases an existing garden may need little (if any) reworking to make it more contemplative for Zen purposes.

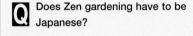

**Q** Does Zen gardening have to be Japanese?

**A** No, although the majority of famous historical Zen gardens are to be found in Japan. In truth, the form is less important than the basis of the design—that is, the way in which the garden is used is more important than what lies within it.

**Q** What about bridges, lanterns, and standing stones?

**A** These are more elements of Chinese and Japanese gardens in general. Though they are used to some degree in a few Zen gardens, it would be wrong to suppose that any of these are crucial to a Zen garden—or even necessary.

**Q** I live in an apartment/condominium complex. Does this mean I must forego this part of the Zen experience?

**A** The size of your garden truly does not matter, as long as you have a good vantage point. Very nice arrangements can be seen on the smallest balconies imaginable.

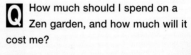

**Q** How much should I spend on a Zen garden, and how much will it cost me?

**A** Spend a lot of effort—as much as you can to create your own vision. Spend as much money as will make you comfortable.

**Q** How big does a Zen garden have to be?

**A** Perhaps we should rephrase the arrangement as a "natural viewing space" rather than as a "garden." Make it as big as you please, or as small as you want—a single flower in a pot, or your entire yard. The one is as fulfilling as the other.

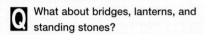

**Q** Does every Zen practitioner have to have a garden?

**A** Not at all. The creation of a garden will not make you a better practitioner of Zen, while the absence of one will not work to your detriment.

**Q** What's wrong with my garden the way it is?

**A** Perhaps nothing, beyond the way in which you view and use it. Splash paint on the garage floor and it's a mess. Do so intentionally on a canvas or wall and it's art.

# 7 Zen, the Self, and Others

Many of us have a hard time dealing with issues of faith. Our society's secular humanism, based on the scientific method, and our inbuilt skepticism prevent us from swallowing any philosophy whole. We want proof—or at least reassurance—and we want it grounded in modern, scientific terminology. Unfortunately, to Zen Buddhists, words are hindrances—not aids—to understanding.

## The psychology of Zen

Even though we might be fascinated by tales of satori and eager to try Zen out, we tend to shy away from it because we think that it is unscientific. For many people, psychology and psychotherapy have replaced philosophy and religion as vehicles for self-understanding. It is therefore natural for us to ask: how do meditative techniques used in Zen practice "work?" More narrowly, can we understand psychologically what is happening in the mind of a Zen practitioner? Is it possible to understand satori in scientific terms?

On one level such questions contradict the main thesis of Zen, which is: just sit. Don't analyze; don't ask; don't second-guess: just sit! But since we live in a skeptical age and are afraid of blind adherence to any doctrine (and rightfully so), attempts have been made to answer them.

**Left** Trying to analyze the psychology of Zen seems to contradict the very principles of the philosophy, which is to just sit and stop analyzing. However, some studies have attempted to investigate how Zen works.

**Right** Not everyone can be a Zen monk. Fortunately, Zen can work for you at any level of commitment.

One of the classic texts is *Zen and the Psychology of Transformation:The Supreme Doctrine* by Hubert Benoit, in which he breaks down the Zen experience and attempts to rebuild it within a Western philosophical context. More recently *Zen and the Brain* by James H. Austin investigated the actual neurochemistry of Zen by means of experiments on practitioners' brains. Seek out these books for a more detailed analysis.

## Levels of Zen practice

For present purposes, we can say that Zen works on our brains on three levels. In order of increasing depth, these are:

- As a relaxation technique
- As a way of grounding ourselves emotionally
- As a way of seeking greater and more direct spiritual connection.

Much work has been done in the last four decades on the benefits of zazen and meditation in dealing with stress. The brain enters a relaxed state (as evidenced by different brainwave signals), which resembles neither regular waking nor sleeping. Scientists continue to investigate these "trance" states, which occur at many different levels of intensity.

At the next level, as we calm our "monkey-minds" and allow the mental mud to settle, our minds naturally turn inward; we move beyond simple relaxation to a state where we are capable of some emotional insight. Modern psychotherapeutic techniques that incorporate Zen and other meditation traditions operate on this level.

It is important to note here that a committed Zen Buddhist who experiences such intense emotional states treats them not as therapeutic breakthroughs but as makyo, or visions, which—despite their value on one level—are actually obstacles to be overcome. This is because the ultimate goal of Zen practice is not mental health, as Westerners understand it, but satori. At the deepest level, Zen is not really about psychology, but about spirituality. If in your sitting (especially if you sit on your own) you find yourself constantly beset by past emotional trauma, you should seek counseling, since few people have the resources to deal with this on their own.

This is not to say that Zen practitioners cannot be concerned with mental health. Many therapists use zazen; many roshi are therapists. The goals of each are not contradictory. Indeed, one cannot follow the precepts without a great deal of empathy, respect for life, and resilience—and surely anyone who exhibits these characteristics would be considered mentally healthy by any standard.

## Zen Buddhism and psychotherapy

Since the dawn of modern psychology in the nineteenth century, Westerners have looked to the East for inspiration. Sigmund Freud and Carl Jung both wrote about Buddhism, and their successors' interest in it has only deepened. By the early 1970s books such as *The Relaxation Response*, *Focusing*, and *Biofeedback* were bestsellers that introduced many Westerners to meditative techniques outside a Buddhist context. Since then writers like Jack Kornfield, Mark Epstein, and John Kabat-Zinn have attempted to fuse Buddhist philosophy with Western psychotherapeutic models. Even the Japanese have joined in the fray, with Morita and Naikan therapies (*see page 97*).

Possibly you have read one or more of these authors, or you may have even undergone therapy using their techniques. What you should understand is that most of these Zen-therapy hybrids are more therapy than Zen. Since the days of Baba Ram Das' (Richard Alpert's) saying "Be Here Now," complex Buddhist philosophy has often been reduced to bite-sized slogans that can be absorbed quickly—and forgotten just as easily. Even some therapists who are Zen practitioners themselves use Buddhist doctrine as a tool for therapy, rather than the other way around.

If you are shopping around for useful bits and pieces that you can use constructively in your own life, that is one thing. If, on the other hand, you wish to become a serious Buddhist, then you are better off sticking to one branch, one school, one roshi. There are inevitable conflicts between Zen Buddhism and modern psychotherapy, and your roshi and your therapist will offer different paths; you cannot expect to follow both simultaneously.

" *Be Here Now.* "

BABA RAM DAS

# Zen and grief

A Buddhist understands that attachment is the source of all misery. The misery that arises when attachment is broken off by separation or death can be crippling. Grief is one of the most powerful emotions—if not *the* most powerful—that we experience. Zen and zazen can help us through the stages of grief. The Zen student has a heightened awareness that all thought and emotion is transient, and is thus less likely to be gripped by feelings of seemingly never-ending sadness. By allowing sad thoughts, regrets, and other emotions to flow through his or her consciousness without fixating on any one in particular, the student experiences the necessary stages of grief and heals quickly.

One well-known story about the Buddha relates how he helped a bereaved mother overcome her grief concerning the loss of her child. The woman was wandering the streets of her town with the dead child in her arms, asking for "medicine" to save her child. The Buddha told her that he knew of a medicine to help her, but first she had to collect a handful of mustard seeds, each one from a house that had not seen death. As she moved from house to house unable to collect the seeds, she realized that death in general—and the death of her child in particular—was a reality.

To our eyes, the Buddha's "therapy" may seem to be unnecessarily harsh, but some modern therapists have drawn parallels between his "mustard-seed" technique and rational-emotive therapy. Confronting the reality of death can be used to overcome grief.

As a student of Zen, you do not repress your emotions. On the contrary, you experience grief to its fullest, but do not let it take over your life or use it as an excuse to mistreat others.

**Above** The Buddha taught that all life is suffering. Once we realize this, we can begin to transcend it. Pain, suffering, and grief don't disappear; we merely accept them for what they are: fleeting images on an imaginary screen.

## Mixing Zen with other philosophies (and religions)

Most Westerners belong to faiths that arose in the Middle East during the period 2000 B.C.E.–800 C.E. People brought up following these faiths may be interested in practicing Zen but afraid of violating precepts of their ancestral religion. Is there a conflict? Can you be a good Jew, Christian, or Muslim and still study Zen?

Both the Jewish and Christian faiths include mystical traditions that discuss "direct experience" of divine truths and incorporate contemplative practice; furthermore, these traditions are a lot less dualistic and more inclusive than your typical fundamentalist might realize. Thus some people who start out interested in Zen end up by turning back to their own mystical traditions. For them, the faiths of their forefathers provide enough nourishment.

Others, such as Rodger Kamenetz in *The Jew in the Lotus,* have written at length about attempts at a basic fusion of Buddhist and Western beliefs (in his case, Judaism). The problem with this is that Western faiths are theistic, whereas Buddhism (and Zen in particular) is iconoclastic and, at heart, not a religion at all but a philosophy.

Jewish and Christian ritual and belief is often tied up with attachment and memory; Jewish and Christian holy days often mark events involving death or loss. The Zen Buddhist calendar also includes celebrations of the birth and death of the Buddha and other major figures. It is difficult to reconcile this with a Buddhist attitude of nonattachment. However, Buddhism at heart is experiential and nonjudgmental, encouraging adherents to try all paths, whereas Judaism and Christianity place more stress on study of scripture and obedience.

**Below** There are many who believe that the ideas of compassion in Christ's teachings may stem from Eastern religions and the teachings of Buddha, Zhuangzi, and others.

On the other hand, since Zen does not involve worship of a deity, and since following the precepts does not require breaking any commandments or laws, some people do bridge the gap. For them, investigating other religions—far from weakening their faith—confirms their own, by holding up a mirror from another perspective. Not all people, though, find it so easy to reconcile the demands of two seemingly disparate belief systems. They may end up choosing to cut the cord with their ancestral faith and community.

If you belong to a congregation and decide to become a student of Zen, talk to your priest, pastor, faith leader, or rabbi—if you haven't already—to discuss your decision and what implications (spiritual or otherwise) you can expect to face. Depending on your denomination, your faith leader may be receptive to the idea of you "trying out" Zen Buddhism while remaining a member of the congregation.

To return to the question at the start of this section: the degree of conflict between Zen and your ancestral faith depends on your level of belief and your flexibility. Some people will feel they have to choose; others will find ways of reconciling Zen with the religion of their forefathers.

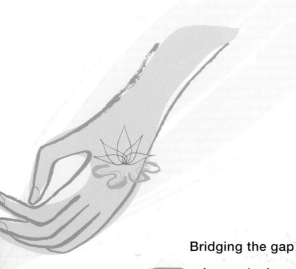

### Bridging the gap

An example of someone who drew from two traditions, found parallels, and experienced no contradiction in belonging simultaneously to both is Father Robert E. Kennedy, a Catholic priest who is also a Zen priest and a student of Yamada Roshi. In *Zen Spirit, Christian Spirit* Kennedy writes that Yamada often told him that he did not want to make him a Buddhist, but simply to "empty" Kennedy, in imitation of Christ, who emptied himself, poured himself out, and clung to nothing. Kennedy thought: *"This Buddhist might make a Christian of me yet!"*

> " *This Buddhist might make a Christian of me yet!* "
>
> FATHER ROBERT E. KENNEDY

## How Zen affects interpersonal relationships

As a follower of the precepts, you abstain from theft, lack of chastity, lying, speaking ill of others, praising yourself, giving spiritual or material aid grudgingly, and anger (among other things). If you align yourself with the Buddha's path, you will find that people will naturally be drawn to you, attracted by your trustworthiness, reliability, and helpful nature. Equally obviously, paying lip service to the precepts while covertly following your own agenda will ultimately accrue enough bad karma to bring about your downfall. No one likes a hypocrite.

By diligently performing zazen, the Zen student becomes more grounded and less excitable. Instead of getting carried away by the brain's powerful bursts of emotion, you will find consciousness settling deep in your belly (*hara* in Japanese). You will become more resilient, able to withstand the shocks and strains of life. *"The willow that bends but does not break"* is one emblematic Zen image. A modern equivalent that will be understood by people of a certain age is the toy known as the Weeble (which is similar to the ancient Japanese round-bottomed toy known as a Daruma)—"Weebles wobble but they don't fall down" was their slogan.

The student of zazen is used to letting thoughts and emotions flow past without unnecessary worry. Knee-jerk reflex behavior is thus short-circuited over time, and you will find that other people are less able to "push your buttons." Unhealthy habits—and relationships—tend to become exposed for what they are: unnecessary attachments. The practitioner finds the inner resources to break these negative cycles and subvert the dynamics that had allowed them to flourish.

**Left** Even this happy-looking couple has problems. To Zen Buddhists, happiness should be enjoyed for what it is, in the moment. Clinging to good times and good memories only brings suffering.

## Coping with hostility

It is possible, unfortunately, that your partner will remain hostile to your study of Zen. This could be because of deep-rooted religious beliefs, which he feels are irreconcilable with Zen Buddhism—or simply because he finds it too "New Age." Relationships can continue under these circumstances, but it will not be easy.

## Living with a nonpractitioner

You may be discovering Zen at a time in your life when you are single or living alone. In this case, making changes in your life and living space is constrained only by your own degree of commitment. However, you may be in a relationship with someone who is not currently interested in Zen. There is potential for conflict here—but it can be avoided, using the precepts.

While it is natural for you to be excited by your new spiritual path, the same may not be true of your roommate or partner. Commitment is one thing; zeal is quite another. If all of a sudden you start chiding him for his attachment to material things, or condescendingly telling her to "just let go of anger," you deserve all the bad karma you will accumulate. If your partner shows any interest, then by all means share. If not, the wisest path is to illuminate the way forward by example (*see page 97*). The onus is on you to be flexible, since you are the one introducing change into the living situation.

In an ideal world, your partner will find that your spiritual commitment has turned you into a better roommate/boyfriend/girlfriend/mate, and will want to find the same spiritual groundedness and to begin walking along the same path. Or, at least, they will come to tolerate and appreciate your devotion.

**Far left** The Zen saying "the willow that bends but does not break" is epitomized by the resilient Daruma toy. These round toys are common in Japan, painted in a folk style. Traditionally, one eye is painted in at the beginning of a quest or undertaking and the second painted upon completion.

## Zazen in groups

Many people discover Zen on their own through books like this one, and then begin zazen on their own. Some people prefer to continue to sit zazen alone, joining (in spirit, anyway) an honorable line of hermits who through the ages have pursued satori in caves and ramshackle huts, far from the beaten track and contact with other people.

**Below** Sitting zazen in groups allows sitters to draw strength and encouragement from each other, whereas those sitting alone might give up.

*" Externally keep yourself away from all relationships, and internally have no pantings in your heart; when your mind is like unto a straight-standing wall, you may enter into the Path. "*

BODHIDHARMA
470–543 C.E.

Others soon find that—as in any exercise regime—their commitment to zazen weakens in solitude. All of the oldest sangha, or Zen communities, in North America began with small groups of people who were simply tired of struggling on their own and as a result formed informal sitting groups. When people sit zazen together, they lend each other support and amplify each other's power, which can result in several people reaching satori simultaneously! And if your partner or roommate is not willing to accommodate your desire for sitting space in your home, then you will probably have to sit zazen elsewhere, and a group may be the ideal answer.

The chances are that, if you live in a city of more than 100,000 people, there is at least one such informal sangha nearby. The larger the city, the more likely it is that this group has established a Zen "community center," or has even affiliated itself to a Buddhist temple with a roshi.

If you have begun to sit zazen and are seeking like-minded people, you could try the following sources of information:

Your local *Yellow Pages* under "Religious Organizations"

A local bookstore or health food store; they usually have bulletin boards that carry advertisements for local Zen groups or centers

An alternative newspaper (if your city publishes one); you might try perusing their advertising section or even calling them up for information

The Internet, which now provides worldwide access for people seeking "cyber-sanghas"; you will find some good web site links to check out on pages 140–141.

One perhaps unlikely place to look for zazen-mates is at your own church, temple, or synagogue (if you are so affiliated). Your congregation may contain like-minded people who are interested in broadening their spiritual approach. Your faith leader may be able and willing to put you in touch with others who are keen to incorporate zazen into their existing devotions.

### Group routines

Some groups meet weekly; others daily. Some sit for half an hour at a time; others for an hour. Some groups are informal, sitting around a table or in someone's living room; others have adopted the full regime of Buddhist ritual, including bowing, incense, and chanting. When you join an existing group, you will by necessity have to meet their schedule and fall in with their plans, although most groups are willing to accommodate a dedicated novice. If, however, you are starting a new group with friends and fellow seekers, it is important that everyone agrees on a schedule—and sticks to it (*see* Chapter 10 for further discussion on finding, joining, and building Zen communities).

# Zen, the Self, and Others
## 10 Questions & Answers

**Q** Has any scientific basis for Zen been found?

**A** None of the Buddha's hypotheses about reality and life have been proven using scientific methods. Of course, the same can be said about most (if not all) religions.

**Q** Has any scientific basis for zazen been found?

**A** Here there has been some progress. Many studies have been done on meditation (including zazen) showing that it is beneficial in reducing stress and increasing emotional stability.

**Q** What is the Relaxation Response?

**A** This refers to a "non-Buddhist zazen" method of stress relief developed by Dr. Herbert Benson of the Harvard Medical School in the 1970s and popularized in his book of the same name.

**Q** What is focusing?

**A** Focusing is a therapeutic technique developed during the 1960s by Dr. Eugene Gendlin, a student of the pioneering American psychologist Carl Rogers. It uses meditative practice to develop a body sense that helps patients to articulate and solve difficult emotional problems. Dr. Gendlin's book *Focusing* is a good place to start if you are interested.

**Q** What is biofeedback?

**A** Biofeedback was originally a general concept for the way all living things use sense-data to self-correct their physiological processes. Starting in the early 1960s, biofeedback techniques using EEG and EMG monitors were used to change brain wave production, heartbeat, and blood pressure in order to reduce stress.

**Q** What is Morita therapy?

**A** This therapy was invented by Dr. Shoma Morita of Japan in the early twentieth century. It combines Western-style therapy with Zen-style "projects" to help patients create mindfulness, focus away from their personal traumas, and begin healing.

**Q** What is Naikan therapy?

**A** Naikan therapy was developed by Iishin Yoshimoto in the 1950s as a tool for personal growth. It is a short-term treatment that involves a chronological review of your life in relation to a parental figure or significant other.

**Q** How can I interest my partner in Zen?

**A** Lead by example and your partner's interest should follow. Far from proselytizing, keep your practice to yourself. Do not sit zazen in your partner's presence; you will only be distracted. Avoid leaving Zen books (even this one!) lying around. Be patient; a wait-and-see attitude is best.

**Q** I have begun zazen, but am unsure about approaching my faith leaders. How can I discuss it with them?

**A** If your religious leader is interested in different paths to spiritual truths, you can approach this from a standpoint of deepening your understanding of your faith. Emphasize that Buddhism is more a philosophy than a religion, and that it does not require you to worship other gods. Link zazen to contemplative traditions within your own faith.

**Q** I am grieving for a loved one and find zazen hard; my mind is flooded with feelings of loss. What can I do?

**A** The traditional response would be to continue sitting and allow these feelings to pass—eventually they will. Today, however, a modern roshi would encourage you to seek counseling and moderate (or even temporarily cease) zazen if it gets too painful for you.

# 8 Zen at Play

The activities of Zen can help us to open the mind to the possibility of Enlightenment by allowing us to be truly "no-mind" (*mu-shin*) and become immersed without focusing.

## Becoming absentminded

The problem is like being in a tense social setting and trying to look casual—the more you try to seem relaxed, the more nervous you appear. If you concentrate on clearing your mind, you cannot clear it because you are concentrating. By absorbing the body in activities in which the movements are practiced, repeated, and eventually become second nature, the mind may find that opening in which you are no longer really concentrating because the body has taken over. It is like trying to become absentminded in a controlled way.

> *Oh how marvelous,*
> *Oh how miraculous,*
> *I gather firewood and*
> *draw water.*
>
> PANG-YUN
> CHINESE POET
> 740–808 C.E.

"The way to the goal is not to be measured. Of what importance are weeks, months, years?"

"But what if I have to break off [the training] halfway?"

"Once you have grown truly egoless you can break off at any time. Keep on practicing that."

"And so we began again from the very beginning, as if everything I had learned hitherto had become useless."

Eugen Herrigel, *Zen in the Art of Archery*

**Left** In *kyudo* (Japanese archery) hitting the bull's-eye is not as important as spiritual and formal preparation. If the actions and mindset are correct, hitting the target is unavoidable.

## The way of the toothbrush

You can already achieve this state to some extent. Imagine it is almost time for bed. You walk to the bathroom to brush your teeth. You pick up the toothpaste tube and your toothbrush in sequence: one always comes first. The toothbrush stays in your hand, or gets placed in a glass, or on the counter, or in your mouth. You know instinctively how many times to turn the toothpaste cap before it comes off. You probably start brush-

ing on the same side each and every time. The chances are that the number of strokes is the same each time before you change the position of the brush. This activity can be done almost completely without concentration because it is repeated daily (the dentist hopes more than once) and because the pattern of steps is the same every time. Most of us are thinking about something else while this is going on—about work or family problems, about what time the meeting is tomorrow morning, or whether the alarm clock has already been set. The body has taken over, allowing the mind to do other things. Concentrate on the activity and, when the body takes over, the mind can clear itself.

*"Release of the arrow should be as if the string has snapped. The bow does not realize; I also do not realize. This is important. Beginners must try to reach this state by drawing the bow and aiming with the aah breath and releasing in time with the umm sound.*

*Breathing for beginners is too fast, or they hold their breath. It comes and goes in gasps and spurts, and training is necessary to overcome this. This also applies to the arts—unless breathing is mastered, the art is not mastered. Though a man may shoot successfully, if the breath is uneven he cannot be called a master."*

The Yoshida School Manual of Archery, sixteenth century

**Left** Kyudo, or the way of the bow, is perhaps one of the most representative of martial arts imbued with Zen thought. Form and control result from direct instruction with a master and years of discipline.

## What are Zen activities?

Traditional Japanese Zen activities include (but are not limited to) calligraphy, painting, swordsmanship, archery, and the tea ceremony—the prerequisite accomplishments of the nobility during the feudal era. (To a lesser degree *No*— a masked drama that is heavily imbued with Zen esthetic— along with gardening and certain forms of poetry are considered to be very much influenced by Zen, although they do not offer the same structure and discipline as the afore- mentioned activities.) The similarities between these activities are not immediately apparent, but elements of each of them are representative of Zen practice. Each is essentially a solitary activity, although they may be practiced in a group; each requires instruction by a master in an oral tradition; each has very set forms that must be followed, and the goal is not as simple as it might appear.

If you practice Western archery as a sport and can hit the target most of the time, you are considered a successful archer. However, Japanese *kyudo* (the way of the bow, using a seven-foot-long bamboo and rattan bow) takes a Zen approach to learning archery and is more concerned with the mental and formal preparation needed to release the arrow than it is with hitting the actual target. If all the preparatory steps have been performed properly, the arrow should strike the target correctly, but the practitioner is not concentrating on the bull's-eye, but rather on the form. The number of steps to the shooting position, the stance, posture, hand positions, grip, focus of sight, angle, number of arrows to be shot, timing, and so on are all prescribed and must be followed. Eventually the actions become second nature: one less thing on which to concentrate.

> " *If you do not spontaneously Trust yourself sufficiently, You will be in a frantic state, Pursuing all sorts of objects And being changed By those objects, Unable to be independent.* "
>
> LIN-JI
> ZEN MASTER
> ?–866 C.E.

## Freeing the mind

Traditional Zen activities may seem extremely rigid in their approach to perfection and their attention to minute details, but it is only through repetition and set patterns that eventually the body is allowed to take over and free the mind from concentration. In the tea ceremony the placement of utensils around the practitioner is planned for ergonomic reasons: those that are used most often are closer to hand, and a set space is required between each piece to avoid knocking things over or hitting them in passing. In the beginning, it seems an enormous bother to remember that the tea caddy should be a hand's breadth to the right of the tea bowl and that the cloth must be folded and placed to the left of the left knee. In time, however, the practitioner knows exactly where things should be, because they are always there and they always return to that position. One less point to remember.

The intricate details of every Zen activity cannot be mastered all at once and each lesson should result in the mastery of one more detail; good teachers will draw and limit the focus to just one element per lesson, even though the entire tea ceremony, practice of the bow, or karate *kata* (pattern exercise) is carried out.

**Left** The tea ceremony as seen from the guest's mat is like a dance of the hands. Each piece has a prescribed placement and usage. The experienced tea master even matches breathing with actions.

## Japan's affinity for the transmission of art

In the same way that Zen has always relied on the direct transmission of knowledge, so the majority of cultural and artistic institutions in Japan have been based on the master/disciple relationship. Whether it be the tea ceremony, sword making, lacquer art, ceramics, dance, *kabuki* theater, or painting, learning has always been reliant on a long period of apprenticeship in the art and, in almost all cases, there is a traditional "foundation"—a basic level of mastery that is expected—before the learner is permitted to begin finding his or her own style or manner. In brush painting, this basic level begins with painting bamboo, orchid, plum, and chrysanthemum, in the depiction of which all the techniques of painting are to be found. The art of calligraphy begins with learning the various strokes and stroke combinations of the clerical script, before moving on to any other style.

### Passing on the heritage

Some arts are passed on in families in such a way that the tradition is never lost, the secrets and direction being handed down to the family head, generation after generation. The Urasenke school of tea is led by the fifteenth head in direct descent from Sen Rikyu, the seventeenth-century master who codified modern "teaism." The raku lineage of potters is similarly led by a fourteenth-generation master. In this way one school maintains the conservative approach to the continuation of the art—that is, keeping the old forms alive—while others are free to pursue their own interpretation.

**Right** A long period of apprenticeship is fundamental to mastering all Japanese Zen activities from calligraphy to the tea ceremony. Calligraphy requires a balance of control and spontaneity. The contemporary style of this lacquered tea caddy translates the traditional motifs of crests and ginkgo leaves into an abstract design.

# The martial arts

Martial arts have also followed this tradition of transmission from master to disciple. Since the beginning of the feudal age in Japan in the twelfth century, heroes have always gone in search of legendary masters of archery or swordsmanship to try and apprentice themselves and learn their secrets. The relation between Buddhism and the fighting arts in Japan is based largely on the concept of the evanescence of life and the temporary nature of existence. This helped to prepare warriors for the eventual, and glorified a death in battle as the inevitable end. The connection with Zen had more to do with the Zen approach to learning and orthodoxy. Stripped of ceremony and the ornate trappings of court Buddhism, Zen was a metaphor for the essence of success in study and practice of fighting. The search for truth in Zen was like the search for the perfect attack or defense.

Repetition of forms and movements is seen in set kata that are practiced in all the martial arts of Japan—*iaido* (sword play), *jodo* (stick fighting), *kendo* (fencing), *karatedo* (weaponless fighting), and *kyudo* (archery). As movement and reaction become second nature to the practitioner, so the body takes over from the mind, which is no longer concerned with thoughts of death or survival, success or failure. Perfect non-thinking reaction is the goal. An example of this was shown by the famous swordsman, poet, artist, and Zen adept Miyamoto Musashi (1584–1645), whose dueling stance was termed "open on all eight sides," a two-sword attitude that leaves the opponent no discernible attack position. His fame and ability were developed to the point where he stopped using swords in fighting duels and adopted wooden staves in order to even his opponents' chances.

**Above** *Karatedo* is based on the exercises devised by Chinese Buddhist masters of the Shao-lin Temple. Aikido, judo, jujitsu, and weaponry stem from fighting technique.

## Froth of the liquid jade

The tea ceremony is perhaps one of the most misunderstood, and yet most complex, of social pastimes, and though there are beverage-related social customs in virtually every culture, almost none has taken etiquette, tradition, and ritual to such a high degree as Zen. From the earliest development of the tea ritual, it has had a close connection with Zen (the legend of the miraculous origin of tea plants has them sprouting from the fallen eyelids of Bodhidharma, who cut them off to stop himself from sleeping during zazen). What began as a practical ritual of passing powdered tea in large bowls to monks, prior to zazen, developed over the centuries into formalized manners and methods for the making and serving of tea. Its greatest masters have inevitably been priests, a tradition that is carried on even today, with the heads of all the major tea schools being Buddhist, if not Zen, priests.

**Below** Two very decorative tea bowls that maintain Zen sensibility in decoration—a reclusive hut, cherry blossom, and leaves falling into a river.

In essence, the tea ceremony is nothing more than the preparation and serving of tea in a prescribed manner. The "modern" tea ceremony grew out of court-style ceremony and was "codified" into its present form by Sen Rikyu (a Zen priest/monk and tea master) in the late sixteenth century at the end of the Japanese Civil War era. As tea master to two successive warlords who controlled almost all of Japan, his taste, opinion, and philosophy became the standards for tea ceremony. He was responsible for both the material culture (gardens, tea huts, bowls, utensils, calligraphy, and so on) and the philosophy of "tea-ism" or *sado* (the way of tea), which is of greater interest to our present discussion. This philosophy boils down (forgive the pun) to two main precepts:

- Sensitivity to doing something correctly
- Sensitivity to a sense of balance or harmony in everything that is done.

When asked about the secret of tea, Sen Rikyu replied in a classic Zen-style response:

**Left** Legend has it that tea sprang from Bodhidharma's eyelids, which he cut away in order to remain awake during zazen.

> " *It is only this… First make the water boil, then infuse the tea, drink it properly; that is all you need to know. If anyone here knows this already, I shall be happy to become his student.* "

## Form and harmony

Doing something correctly in the tea ceremony really means doing it in the prescribed way, considering each movement, each placement, each choice. Like a choreographed dance, each movement has been set down by tradition, for both practical reasons and reasons of taste. For instance, let's look at the example of taking the lid off the kettle: the right hand places the folded napkin on the lid (too hot to handle directly), the lid knob is gripped with the thumb and two fingers (it's small), the lid is raised two inches off the kettle (allowing the steam to escape), then tilted downward for three seconds (allowing condensation to drip back into kettle); next the lid is drawn toward the body and placed on the lid rest, at the corner below the kettle (moving it directly from the kettle to the stand will cause your kimono sleeve to fall in the fire).

In time you will begin to draw these elements into your everyday life, in the way you handle chopsticks, pour tea, or pick up a rice bowl. Form is not everything, however, and a sensitivity to doing things correctly also means deciding on priorities and goals in an activity.

At a basic level, the sense of harmony can be as simple as the choice of a brightly decorated bowl with a more subdued tea caddy; a balance of light with dark; a sincerity in expending a great deal of effort, but little expense. For example, heavy things should be handled in such a way that they seem light, and light as if they were heavy. In summer you should try to evoke a sense of coolness, and in winter a sense of warmth.

**Above** Any Zen activity is about balance and harmony—contrast bright or light colors with darker, more subdued tones.

### Sen Rikyu's opinion

After a certain tea gathering in which his colleagues criticized the host for being clumsy and inattentive to form in his preparation, Sen Rikyu thought the opposite and that the minor mistakes of the host were due to his desire to serve the large number of guests efficiently; they were not inappropriate, but harmonious.

## One encounter, one opportunity

More important still is the balance between host and guest, summed up in the Japanese term *ichi-go, ichi-e* (one encounter, one opportunity). At a meeting, both host and guest have responsibilities toward each other, and in the tea ceremony (and to a degree in Japan in general) this means that the hosts provide as best they can in the way of refreshments and entertainment, using their good plates, displaying household treasures, and expending a little extra effort. The guest's responsibilities, on the other hand, include appreciating what is provided, taking care with the host's good plates, and obliging or entertaining the host.

**Right** Both host and guest have a responsibility to the success of a meeting. A traditional scene greeting Japanese guests, tea and sweets are often prepared just in advance of the guests' arrival in homes, offices, inns, and temples.

### Sen Rikyu and the joker

One story has Sen Rikyu on his way to drink tea at the home of a practical joker. Along the garden path he encounters a large pit, poorly disguised with bamboo leaves. Rikyu obligingly jumps into the pit and his host arrives with profuse apologies. He leads Rikyu to a bath already prepared and a change of clothes and then into the tea room. Had Rikyu avoided the pit, the meeting would have been less than perfect in the mind of the host.

## Zen and journaling

For as long as writing has existed, people have kept records of their daily lives, or diaries containing their inner thoughts and secrets. You may be one of these people. You may not realize it, but if you do keep a journal, you are performing a kind of practice that, with a few changes, could complement or even supplement your zazen.

Natalie Goldberg has written several books investigating the causal link between Zen and journaling—with the specific intention of "liberating the author within" and overcoming internal obstacles to writing. Her first book, *Writing Down the Bones*, has become a bestseller, and she has written several sequels. Her journaling is not the Samuel Pepys-type record of daily life; rather, it is almost a kind of written zazen. It offers a great way to overcome writer's block, which inevitably arises when your "inner critic" suffocates your creative urge with niggling doubts and pessimism. In *Writing Down the Bones* Goldberg lists the seven rules that govern journaling as zazen:

Keep your hand moving. Don't stop writing, no matter what. If you give yourself 10 minutes a day for journaling, you should be writing the entire time.

Lose control. Say exactly what you want to say, without worrying about political correctness, self-image, or "who might read this."

Be specific. Get beyond labels and superficial adjectives; use all your senses in describing people, objects, and feelings. Say "Kia," not "car"; "PBS documentary on lizards," not "television show."

Don't think. Don't critique, don't second-guess, above all don't stop. Just go with the flow; start with the first thing that comes into your head, and go from there.

Don't worry about punctuation, spelling, and grammar. Again, don't get hung up on details. You can always go back later and dig out the nuggets.

You are free to write the worst junk. Give yourself permission to be bad, to fail, to be trite and clichéd—just write.

Go for the jugular. Don't circle around uncomfortable topics, if that's what you are writing about. Good writing is hard. Avoid the painful and your writing might be beautiful, but it will also be distant and abstract.

As with zazen, the important thing is to write every day, regardless of whether or not you "feel like it." Ideally, you should write for the same amount of time each day, and Goldberg even goes so far as to advocate using a fountain pen rather than ballpoint, because of the tactile control that this gives you.

Goldberg was a serious Zen student, who studied under Katagiri Roshi and is now ordained herself. Her books detail the deeply spiritual and loving relationship that she had with him—although at one point early on he told her to forget zazen altogether and make writing her practice. This illustrates the basic idea that, whatever you may be passionate about, it can become your practice just as well as, or even better than, sitting zazen.

**Right** Mindfulness is not restricted to sitting; to the practitioner, all things done with attention and focus can be considered zazen. Journaling is just another way to help empty and still the mind.

## The Buddha laughed: Zen and humor

*Dan Xia taking shelter in a Buddhist temple on a cold evening found himself with little fuel for his meager fire and took down one of the Buddha images from the altar and added it to the embers. The temple custodian was appalled by his sacrilege and chastized Dan Xia for his irreverence. Dan Xia calmly took up a stick and began scratching about the embers, and replied: "I am looking for holy relics among the ashes."*

*The puzzled and still furious custodian asked: "How can you get holy relics from a wooden Buddha?"*

*"If there are no relics to be found," replied Dan Xia, "how can this be considered a Buddha, and if not a Buddha, how am I committing any sacriligious act. Would you mind if I added the two remaining Buddhas to my fire?"*

Traditional

More than any other Buddhist school, Zen uses humor to teach and promote understanding, poking fun at itself and the overly serious side of religion and philosophy (a curious habit picked up from Daoist precedent). It can be irreverent, ridiculous, and absurd, but is rarely simplistic or as straightforward as it might at first appear. Take, for example, the story of Siddhartha Gautama and the flower—Maha-kashyapa's smile was irreverent and spontaneous (he is also shown in some images of the "Death of the Buddha" laughing, when everyone else is crying), but the reason for his reaction is not easily understood. Some say it is because he realized that the flower represents life and eventual death, and thus the cycle of reincarnation, which he now understands how to overcome. It may be at that point he comprehended that he was to take over after the Buddha and was laughing nervously. We may never know.

**Above** Humor plays a large role in Zen teaching and activities. Kabuki and No theater masks display a range of emotions.

**Right** Toba Sojo's "Animal Scrolls" were a twelfth-century satire of the clergy of the established Buddhist Church. In later sections, the monkeys are courtiers, while frogs are abbots and high clerics controlling the rabbits.

In many paintings Daikoku, the God of Happiness, appears frequently, as do images of Bodhidharma looking rough and scraggy. One famous work by the *ukiyo-e* (woodblock print) artist Hokusai shows the rough Zen style of painting juxtaposed with the fine woodblock style, in a depiction of Bodhidharma and a courtesan—but the two have switched costumes and painting styles. And the inscription around one circle drawn with a single stroke by the Soto master Zuigaku Renpo goes thus: "Enso [a circle], don't cut nails in dim light." But Zen humor is perhaps most evident in the responses that are given by masters in the course of instruction. Seekers of wisdom often receive responses from their masters that appear nonsensical or completely unrelated to the instruction that they seek.

*A novice once spoke to Joshu saying, "I have newly entered the community of your temple. Please instruct me."*

*Joshu asked "Have you had breakfast?"*

*The monk replied, "Yes."*

*Joshi said, "If you have, go wash your bowls."*

Traditional

Here is yet another example of Zen humor that may not be quite so simple as it seems at first. The master's instruction may be intended to teach the monk the concept of situation and action—or perhaps the master just likes a tidy monastery. Either way, through a very direct approach that cuts away all explanations, Joshu gets to the kernel of meaning.

# Zen at Play

## 10 Questions & Answers

**Q** Do I have to take up Japanese hobbies such as karate and the tea ceremony?

**A** The number of activities that can be approached in this way is endless. You will find, however, that it is difficult to adapt activities in which you need to depend on working with others, such as team sports. Skill activities, especially those with repetitive actions and a definable goal, are best suited to Zen students.

**Q** Are some activities more Zen than others?

**A** Those activities that require skill and concentration instead of relying on chance are more readily adaptable. A good example is golf: although the outcome of each shot is not entirely predictable, increased skill leads to greater success, and the actions and movements are repetitive.

**Q** I like to have fun when I'm immersed in hobbies and sports. Will I lose my enjoyment?

**A** Anything you do can be approached in a Zen manner. Think of a piano player whose hands fly across the keys without much thought. This might seem enjoyable, but imagine if piano playing were your profession and practicing was necessary rather than voluntary. All things can be approached in different ways—it is just a matter of perspective.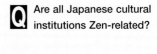

**Q** Are all Japanese cultural institutions Zen-related?

**A** No, but many that developed from the culture of the feudal age are. The literary arts of painting, music, and calligraphy are all connected to Zen, as are the martial arts and the tea ceremony. Certain performing arts such as No theater, classical dance, and some types of drumming have Zen backgrounds or are grounded in Zen philosophy, but are not really considered Zen activities.

**Q** Can cooking be Zen?

**A** Definitely. If you think about it, cooking has all the elements of a traditional Zen activity: required steps that are repeated each time, concentration, a definable goal, a sense of artistry, and it is often passed down from master to disciple. Some cooking activities are particularly Zen in their approach, for example making pastry (the mastery of the steps and methods being essential).

**Q** What is mastery?

**A** Perfectly executed activity, but executed effortlessly and unconsciously, just like the signing of a signature.

**Q** Do I need a master in order to learn?

**A** It is preferable, but not crucial. There are many who have the discipline to approach and dissect an activity in such a way that they can guide their own progress, but others who find their way much more easily with someone to nudge them in the correct direction. A roshi can add entirely new facets to your study.

**Q** Isn't experience the best teacher?

**A** We would say it is, but does it all have to be your own? Frustration at not advancing can be a terrible detriment, especially as we place such a premium on time in the modern world. If you play golf and never take a lesson, you may eventually become a great golfer, but even natural talent can be improved by the advice of others.

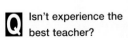

**Q** Is there a contradiction between the peaceful nature of Buddhism and Zen practice of the martial arts?

**A** Not really, for in the present day this is more sport than killing technique. Martial arts are particularly well suited as Zen activities because they are fast-paced, physical, require intense concentration and control, and yet are very regimented. In fact Chinese *gong-fu*, karate, and other fighting arts trace their origins to the Shao-lin Temple-style of boxing, originally developed as an aid to mental and physical discipline.

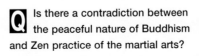

**Q** What in Zen, and Zen activities, is fun?

**A** Zen offers great freedom to "thumb your nose" at order, dogma, and rules. Sen Rikyu's "tea-ism" was a modernized response to ritualized court tea ceremony, while calligraphy has traditional set forms and styles that Zen calligraphers sought to unseat through wildness, boldness, and spontaneity.

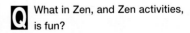

# 9 Zen Design

In the modern world of popular culture, where image and labels seem to overpower substance in importance, the adjective "Zen" gets bandied around to describe almost anything that is Asian-inspired. A black-leather sectional sofa in an almost bare room is "Zen"; three small scallops on a plate with a dollop of dark sauce and two chives is "Zen"; a little rock sculpture with a burbling water pump is "Zen."

## Everything stark, dark, and simple

What is it about Zen, that the term can be used to evolve imagery across such a diverse field? What connects these images to zazen and satori? Where does "Asian-inspired" end and "Zen" begin? To answer these questions, we have to look at the context of Japanese and Far Eastern design and extract from this a more educated perspective.

To say that all Japanese art is minimalist, monochromatic, and Zen-inspired would be as incorrect as assuming that all French art is ornate, colorful, and baroque. Each country has had periods in which the taste for art and material goods was garish and lavish, and periods in which it was simple and subdued. In China, taste in many art forms ran according to the dynasty of the time, with Qing being positively garish, representing the Chinese taste as the West knows it best. In Japan, a taste for the subdued has existed since the Ashikaga period in the fourteenth century, but only within one section of society.

**Left** The formal robes worn by the monk suggests the calligraphy is being done as part of a special event, possibly New Year celebrations, an ordination, or special visit.

## Painting: the Song tradition

The style of Chinese landscape painting, particularly on paper with brush and ink, has been highly influential on the development of Zen styles of calligraphy and painting. Subjects are suggested by shape rather than clearly depicted through detail. The tension and tranquility of Song paintings—seen in the balance of crowded and open space, dark and light, curvaceous and straight, asymmetry and off-center focal points—can also be seen in the design of gardens, interiors, ceramics, and other crafts. The monochromatic nature and misty atmosphere of such paintings has also been influential in developing the later tea taste of *wabi-cha* (a style of tea ceremony).The Song literati were responsible for the back-to-nature esthetic that glorified the simple and the rustic—a taste that had a great impact on the development of the tea ceremony and architecture in Japan.

Zen painting differs from other styles of the Chinese tradition in its subject matter and manner of spacing. Many early Chinese works that inspired the Zen style (the twelfth- and thirteenth-century artists Muqi, Liang Kai, and Shide) took the rough brush style of Song landscape and brought the subject focus forward, with just a bare hint of background or no background at all. The figures (in many cases famous Zen adepts or religious subjects) became the focal point, with clothing and faces brought to life through a mix of quickly executed strokes, fine calligraphic details, controlled washes, and varied ink tones. A face and a foot might be very detailed; the robes and body just a few broad lines defining a rough silhouette. Calligraphic works similarly focused on a single character (such as "duality" or "mind") or on just a few (a Zen poem or saying), written in a rough, aggressive style. Many calligraphers of the more formal traditions decried these as unsophisticated.

## Poetry: the art of haiku

In Japan, painting and calligraphy from the sixteenth century onward included two styles in which simplicity was even more highly espoused. One style is best represented by the *enso*: a simple large circle painted in one stroke, around which a commentary would be written; or a single line or a grouping of circle, square, and triangle. Related to this, but less abstract, is the *haiku* style of painting, which matched the popular three-line, 17-syllable poem style with a simple, almost primitive, style of painting. Works of the former style tend to be dogmatic and introspective, while those of the latter style are more light-hearted and humorous with a tinge of Buddhist sentiment and melancholy, as befits the work of a dilettante monk/artist.

Haiku itself merits a bit of exploration as an art form, since it is strongly tied to Zen sentiment. Haiku is one of the last restrictive meter-poetry forms developed in Japan, long after *waka* (31 syllables) and *renga* (linked-verse waka), not to mention Chinese poetic forms popularized in different periods. In three lines, of five, seven, and five characters respectively, the poet sets a scene, describes the action, and creates a broad image, making the poem spiritual or philosophical beyond the first two descriptive lines. It is the last line that is meant to leave the deepest impression, at once reflective of the poem, but resonating with a wider philosophical meaning.

**Above** The classic form of Zen painting and calligraphy together is the enso poem—a quickly executed circle representing nothingness, reincarnation, mind, hara, tea bowl, pond, and so on.

### A classic example by Basho

| | |
|---|---|
| *Furu ike ya* | The ancient pond, ah… |
| *Kawazu tobikomu* | A frog ready to jump in |
| *Mizuno oto* | The sound of water. |

The final line describes no action, but subtly suggests the disappearance of the frog. It also has a spiritual allusion to Buddhist causation: sound causing movement, movement causing ripples, ripples spreading across the water. It reflects a sense inherent in most Japanese art forms, referred to as *mono no aware*—a sense of finiteness, melancholy, loneliness, and emptiness. The poem starts with the frog alone, and ends without even the frog, just the pond alone.

## Design: the empty view

Painting and calligraphy of the "literati" school and Zen traditions in design are even more notable in the influence they have had on the development of spatial balance and harmony. If we take as an example almost any European painting (still life, landscape, or portrait), the focus will probably be on the center of the space, with the view radiating outward horizontally. Van Gogh's "Sunflowers," the "Mona Lisa," and Michelangelo's "School of Athens" all place the visual focus dead center and balance equally both sides (left and right) with activity, figures, or color; space is filled across the entire field. Such symmetry and crowding of space are less esthetically pleasing to Chinese, Japanese, and Korean artists, whose traditions place the areas of focus toward the bottom of the frame and force the view upward, or possibly toward a lower corner of the field, balanced by a line of calligraphy in the opposite upper corner. Large areas of the works are frequently left open, placing further emphasis on the areas of depiction. This balance of space with emphasis in one corner or to one side is predominant in Japanese art and design, as seen in the layout of living space, food, ceramics, and lacquer.

**Below** A haiku-style painting with a poem comparing a frog to the Buddha. Note the calligraphic form of the frog executed in 11 strokes.

**Bottom** Cloud perspective in a Chinese-style painting allows us to understand that the dark humps in the midfield are in fact distant peaks.

## Chanoyu: "hot water for tea"

No institution or movement has influenced Japanese design more than the tea ceremony, largely because it has been an integral means of carrying forward artistic traditions since the fifteenth century. Because the tea ceremony aroused interest in the wealthy and powerful alike (it was part of the education and refinement of a gentleman), and due to the patronage of the most powerful political figures of the time (Sen Rikyu's patrons included Oda Nobunaga, the unifier of the country, and Toyotomi Hideyoshi, later the *kampaku* or political ruler of Japan), the taste of "tea-ism" really became the national taste in matters of design.

Rikyu's tea taste reflected that of the developing merchant class, and just as Zen in its early years represented a partial reaction to the lavishness of the established Buddhist church and court ritual, so Rikyu's codified tea ceremony eliminated much of the pomp and extravagance of the court tea ceremony (stands, trays, and decorative utensil sets, for instance). Elements that he added reflected new traditions of the period, which in time would become commonplace in Japan—*tatami* mats, new ceramic styles (such as *raku* and *oribe*), *tabi* socks, the *kaiseki* meal, for example. His taste was to become the benchmark by which design would be judged, and shape, size, color, material, and use were all to be compared against that which "Rikyu preferred."

**Right** The colorful kimono worn by these young women indicates that this tea gathering is part of Coming of Age ceremonies (January 15). Note the choice of an angular water jar (*left*), which is chosen to offset the roundness of the brazier and kettle (*right*).

Rikyu's taste was based on "balance," a design middle way. Heavy objects are handled as if to appear light and vice versa, and to suggest coolness in summer, warmth in winter. Color is not disdained, but matched with pieces that are less ornate. Seasons, circumstances, and even the weather influenced the esthetics of the tea room.

In the development of *chanoyu* (literally "hot water for tea," the common name for the tea ceremony, as opposed to sado, "the way of tea" or "tea-ism"), Rikyu allowed himself to be guided by two esthetic principles—wabi (refined elegance) and sabi (serenity). Both of these terms have much wider interpretations than their translations suggest and are very difficult to pin down by definition, even in Japanese, although they will become clearer through examples. Perhaps more than any other principles, these two define most closely what is now considered "Zen."

# Wabi

Wabi is a taste for the natural, for what is simple, practical, and without ostentation. A good example is the tea room itself—small, yet comfortable and functional, constructed of plain wood, with straw matting on the floor. The classic and most popular tea room is the size of four tatami mats (approximately three yards square).

As a representative wabi material, bamboo was praised by Rikyu as being eminently suited to the tea ceremony due to its durability, its flexibility, and its adaptability. A simple cylindrical piece of bamboo cut from a mature stalk at the node section serves as a lid-rest; a thinner stalk split vertically along the grain into fine tines down two-thirds of its length becomes a whisk; take a node section and pare down the sides to form a cup; add a length of bamboo as a handle to form a ladle; a simple length of bamboo with a properly bent, flat, wide end becomes a tea scoop. Add to this the flower vase, the ribs of a folding fan, the chopsticks used in the tea ceremony, baskets, and so on and you can begin to appreciate how eminently versatile bamboo is. Although tea scoops are also made of ivory and precious wood, and flower vases from bronze and porcelain, the number of simple bamboo items designated Important Cultural Artifacts and National Treasures in Japan attests to bamboo's status as a material.

**Above and below**
Bamboo is a versatile material and used in Japan for a great many objects, such as chopsticks, fans, and baskets. *Chashaku* (tea ladle, *top left*) and *chasen* (whisk, *top right*) are both crafted ingeniously from bamboo. The ladle comprises only two pieces, the whisk a single section of bamboo split to create tines.

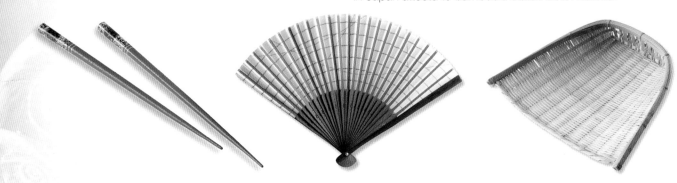

## Sabi

Sabi adds to wabi a sense of melancholy and aloneness (but not necessary "loneliness") that is reminiscent of misty, monochromatic landscape paintings. This explains the Zen preference for an overcast versus a bright and sunny day; for dawn or dusk to noon; for subdued and dark colors over garish and bright ones; for less rather than more. A good example of this is flower arrangement for the tea ceremony (which is different from the more popular ikebana tradition), in which a single camellia or, at most, a few light-colored mountain flowers are arranged naturally in a bamboo or old bronze vase. This offers a stark contrast to Western flower arrangement, in which the predominant image is colorful, symmetrical, and vibrant.

## The taste for wabi-sabi

This can perhaps be best understood from the names that were given to the most famous tea rooms of the seventeenth century—Mugai-an (Introvert Hut), Yu-in (Further Retirement), Kanun-tei (Cold Cloud Arbor), Koho-an (Lone Mugwort Hut), Ichimoku-an (One Tree Hut), and Shogetsu-tei (Pine Moon Arbor). With the tea hut placed in the farthest part of the tea gardens, the practitioner follows a path away from the reality of the outside world into a closed, different world, stopping along the way to wash at a stone basin and to admire the view from other spots along the path. The representation of the Buddhist spiritual journey is here made real, allowing warriors and samurai lords the opportunity to slough off the outside world and thus to become scholar-recluses for the duration of the tea ceremony.

### But what is Zen design?

Like proper Zen masters, we are really answering nothing in this chapter and have painted no clearer picture of Zen design than when we began—perhaps because Zen design (like wabi-sabi) is general enough that its scope will change over time, just as taste changes. A few years ago, we were introduced to a New York City art gallery housed in a newly renovated brownstone building. What was notable was the very insincere-looking tea house that had been constructed in the back garden, out of place as it was in New York City; and yet the interior gallery—with its high white walls, hardwood floors, dark banisters, and low benches—seemed extremely wabi, in that it served its purpose excellently and flooded the paintings with natural light. To us, the modern gallery was more "Zen" than the supposedly Zen tea room.

**Above** Sen Rikyu's Zen-inspired taste for simplicity in the tea ceremony has not waned. Elements, such as the straw tatami mats and the alcove for reflection on the flower arrangement and hanging scroll remain standard in Japanese domestic architecture.

## Ceramics

In ceramics, tea masters prefer vessels that are neither delicate nor highly decorative, but heavy stoneware and other low-fired wares. In keeping with the sense of wabi, pottery used during the tea ceremony tends to be imperfect, rough, and glazed in natural tones of yellow, green, black, and brown—as opposed to the perfect white and bright red-and-blue decoration of the porcelain of the same period. The main ceramic vessel of the tea ceremony is the bowl in which tea is both made and served; with the bamboo tea scoop and the ceramic tea caddy, this represents one of three essential items of the tea master. Suitability for use depends on practical characteristics: its stability on an uneven mat floor; the ease with which it can be held at the side by one hand and in the palm; the presence of a foot-ring that can be gripped with the fingertips when emptying out waste water; a diameter large enough to insert a hand for cleaning.

Native Japanese ceramics were often used in conjunction with imported and older pieces from Song China and Koryo Korea. Chinese wares were the luminous and soft-toned celadons (pottery with a gray green glaze), their forms austere

**Below** The sencha (leaf tea) tea ceremony uses teapots of understated elegant design inspired by Chinese folk wares such as Yixing. Literati poetry extolling the virtues of tea is incised on the sides.

**Left** Tea masters prefer bowls that are subdued and simple in design.

and simple, with clean lines and a minimum of decoration. A straight-sided Jianware bowl in black glaze might have as its only decoration tiny oil spots or brown "rabbit's fur" streaks that occur naturally in the firing process. The beauty of a celadon vase lacking handles and surface decoration of any kind might be concealed in the gentle curves of its sides. Korean ceramics had two extremes of styles, from very fine white to sea-blue celadons and coarse brownware, both of which made an impact on the developing taste of the tea ceremony.

The most sought-after tea bowls, Ido bowls, are in fact early Korean rice bowls that were exported to Japan in the fourteenth and fifteenth centuries, but which possessed the wabi qualities of simplicity, natural color, and texture. Most were thrown by farmers or other tradesmen rather than potters, and have a silhouette characterized by a prominent foot-ring, straight angular sides, and irregularities such as finger marks and glaze fissures. The best examples are noted for a glaze irregularity around the foot-ring, where the glaze has not adhered properly to the ceramic body, causing a creeping and bubbling into little islands, with a texture described as "orange peel."

In court-style tea ceremony, the most coveted bowls were imported twelfth-century Chinese Jianware bowls of oil-spot glaze, hare's-fur glaze, and other poetically named styles.

## Rakuware

Rikyu promoted his own variety of the tea bowl, a ceramicware specially developed for the tea ceremony and now recognized internationally. He commissioned a Korean tile maker who was active in the Kyoto area to produce bowls in a small, back-alley kiln in various squat shapes and dark glaze colors. The resulting bowls were imperfect, with sides that were unevenly smooth and edges that were not straight; however, this low-fired earthenware was porous and light enough to allow bowls of hot tea to be handled more easily than porcelain, which became too hot to the touch. Its tactile qualities and warmth were equated with jade and wood. Rikyu formally presented his tea bowls to his patron Hideyoshi, who was so taken with them that he in turn presented the potter with a gold seal bearing the second character of the Juraku Palace: *raku*—the name by which such low-fired ceramic art is now known.

# Zen Design
## 10 Questions & Answers

**Q** Are Zen design and minimalism synonymous?

**A** No, but simplicity plays a large role in the esthetic of Zen religious art and the products and taste of many arts related to Zen. Envisage a classic painting, "Persimmons" by Mu qi (a thirteenth-century Chinese artist), which comprises six round shapes in a row with perfunctory stems: one very dark, three dark, and two light. They need no table, no shadow, no branch, or even perspective; they are suspended in space—the openness need not be filled.

**Q** If I like color, clutter, and fine things, is my taste non-Zen?

**A** The esthetic principles of wabi-sabi have had an enormous influence on design in Japan. From a quick survey of tea objects, it would be easy to assume that the preference is for dark, rough, old, sparsely furnished, and minimized. However, there is also a love of ornate color. Balance is created by using the ornate and colorful as a focus, rather than as a theme, so highlight the ornate by surrounding it with the more subdued.

**Q** Are Zen design and esthetics only to be found in Japanese design?

**A** The same principles can be found internationally—in the domestic architecture of Frank Lloyd Wright, the early clothing designs of Armani and Perry Ellis, English country gardens, Mission-style furniture, many Arts and Crafts designs of the late Victorian era, and so on.

**Q** I don't like antiques and things I can't use every day. Where can I find modern Zen-inspired pieces?

**A** The guiding principles when choosing furniture and homewares should be functionality and simplicity. Ask: Does this item perform the function that I need it to? Can one item perform dual functions? Will this last or is it easily replaceable? Bamboo was one of the favorite materials of the tea masters as it came in a variety of sizes, was easily worked, renewable, adaptable, waterproof, and strong. Compare and weigh your choices against such characteristics.

**Q** Is something Japanese automatically Zen-inspired?

**A** Definitely not. Japan has as many frivolous, gaudy, luxurious, and impractical products as any other country. However, a lot of Japanese design is Zen-inspired, mainly because simplicity is still considered more appealing. In the West, premodern taste always equated more ornate and richly decorated with more expensive and hence more desirable. In Japan taste has always been the opposite.

**Q** As I become more involved in Zen practice should I try to live without appliances and possessions?

**A** There are many things that we do not necessarily need. But needs can be judged in many different ways, and items around us can have both practical and spiritual benefits. From a Buddhist perspective, objects that make our lives easier are less of an obstacle to Enlightenment than simple items to which we have emotional ties; so keep the dishwasher, if you like.

**Q** Should I get back to nature to be more Zen? Should I move to the country?

**A** If you are a modern person, with a modern job living in a modern city, it would seem both impractical and unnecessary to move to the country, or to try and bring the country to you. In all things, especially in living, there should be balance and sincerity.

**Q** How can I live without clutter? I have so many things I really feel I should keep.

**A** Take a modern Japanese approach to the problem. A great deal of homes are limited in living space, but have good storage space. You don't need to see everything you own all the time. It helps to refresh your appreciation of pieces to forget about them for a while and concentrate on others.

**Q** Is the use of metal undesirable in Zen design?

**A** Excess in anything can be unwise, so overuse of metal is undesirable, but the actual material is not. Cast iron, bronze, and copper are integral to objects used in the tea ceremony. Think of sincerity as well: the gleaming copper surface of a newly made object is more sincere than a newly made object that has been treated, acid-washed, and patinated to look old.

**Q** What really comprises Zen design?

**A** Without defining the subject too clearly, we can say that Zen design is subdued rather than ornate, pragmatic rather than luxurious, tranquil rather than gaudy, aged rather than fresh, somber rather than vibrant, simple rather than complex.

# 10 Moving On

You have almost finished your initial exploration into the world of Zen. The time has come for you to embark on your practice. This chapter can be likened to the final state of Enlightenment: "returning to the marketplace."

## Returning to the marketplace

In this state the seeker, having attained satori and entered the world of no-mind, gradually returns to the world of the here-and-now, integrating Enlightenment into normal daily life. Of course you have not yet attained Enlightenment, but perhaps you have caught a fleeting glimpse of the ox and are curious about what life after satori is like.

People who think that attaining satori will make their life one of permanent bliss are very much mistaken. Nirvana and samsara are one. Enlightened people still have to shovel snow and change diapers; they get angry; they sometimes make poor choices. The difference lies in their view of the world and how they react to it.

**Above** Remember this picture? It is easy for some to remain secluded in the bliss of satori. Monks have even died while sitting zazen. But the Buddha himself returned to the world.

## Moving in and out of practice

The wisest roshis understand that everyone passes through periods of diminished motivation, flagging passion for satori, a weakened will to sit zazen. The traditional response is: "Don't like; don't dislike; don't think—just sit!" In other words, use your feelings as a judoist would use an opponent's weight to throw him to the ground. No spiritual journey worth mentioning comes without obstacles and self-doubt; perseverance is its own reward.

As our lives have become more hectic and our collective spiritual will has weakened, so another response has arisen: "It is natural to move in and out of practice. There is no point in continuing practice if you are not in the right place for it. Better to temporarily discontinue practice and return to it when you are ready, than persist grimly and resent it."

Which of these views is correct? The answer is that the distinction between what is right and what is wrong is artificial—the path that is right for one person is wrong for another. Zen Buddhism has always emphasized the paramount importance of personal experience. Only the seeker can know when zazen no longer provides the necessary nourishment.

As time goes by you will encounter various hurdles: not just the ones that the Buddha faced under the bodhi tree, but ones that he could only imagine. You will move, and your new house will not have a good place to sit zazen; you will begin a relationship with someone who finds your practice "weird" and forces you to choose between them and it; you will begin a new job that has you working 18-hour days; you will give birth to three children and have no time to sit. These are the events that push us in and out of zazen—but Zen practice does not begin and end with formal zazen. Any act can become practice: sweeping, laundry, filing, stacking chairs. Don't become attached to zazen *per se* as the sole vehicle toward Enlightenment. Satori that is confined to the sitting room is small satori indeed. Eventually, you will be able to do zazen on the subway, on the train, or while filling out forms at the post office.

## Overcoming obstacles

If you have begun zazen on your own, you may be struggling with problems such as aching knees and legs, boredom, an inability to focus, drowsiness, and so on. These are normal beginner's obstacles, but you should have the will to persist. If you don't, then you should explore alternate methods of practice, such as journaling (*see pages 108–109*)—or decide that Zen is not, after all, for you.

**Below** As the dew falls from the leaves, so does commitment to enlightenment. But the dew will rise again tomorrow.

## Zen in the community

You may go through periods without doing any serious practice, and yet still consider yourself a student of Zen. Or you may find solitary practice unsatisfying and lonely, in which case there are many sangha that welcome newcomers; these Zen communities enjoy the benefits of like-minded individuals coming together for mutual encouragement and spiritual synergy.

## Zen centers

In the beginning there were a few individuals who had read Watts and Suzuki and wanted to "try out Zen"; these people formed the first informal sangha in the West. By the late 1950s, Zen centers had opened in San Francisco and London. Today, most large and many smaller towns have at least one place where Zen students gather for zazen.

Zen centers can generally be found in the *Yellow Pages* under "Religious Organizations," or in the *White Pages* under Z. Some consist simply of a rented room in a community center, where people congregate to practice zazen; others are fully fledged communities with a resident roshi and full-time employees. Some centers are very "Buddhist" in orientation (and differ according to which tradition and region they draw inspiration from); others are more secular or ecumenical in outlook. Some have adopted all the trappings of the East, including robes, incense, and chanting; others have adapted to Western styles.

If you are lucky enough to live within convenient distance of several centers, you have the luxury of choosing the one that comes closest to your own outlook, but it is more likely that you will have to make do with the one center in your district.

Alternatively—if you have the drive and initiative—you could put up some advertisements locally and set up your own Zen center (*see* Chapter 7).

Centers generally maintain a regular zazen schedule, with sittings in the early mornings (to give people time to get to work) and possibly in the early evenings. Some also organize regular sesshin (*see page 132*). They differ considerably in terms of formality, so that some simply allow people to sit as they like, whereas others conform to traditional ritual.

## Zen temples

The Far East has many famous and beautiful Zen temples, which were often also monasteries where monks lived and devoted their lives to achieving satori. The first Zen Buddhist temples in the West were founded in the early part of the twentieth century by Japanese, Chinese, Korean, and Vietnamese immigrants. By the late 1960s more and more Westerners were beginning to study Zen, and as a result new temples were founded and run by Westerners. If there is a Zen Buddhist temple in your area, it may therefore be a traditional temple with services in, say, Japanese, servicing the remnants of its aging Japanese population. Alternatively, it may be one that has grown with the times, having a Western roshi and functioning almost entirely in English (though using Sanskrit in its services, as the original tongue of worship).

**Left** The solitary figure of a scholar recluse communing with nature is here given a religious undertone by substitution with a *lohan* (or *rakan* in Japanese) or disciple of Buddha. Kano school painting of the early nineteenth century.

### Defining satori

Although words cannot tell you about satori, any more than a picture of an orange can tell you what it tastes like, two Zen sayings attempt to answer this question:

• **"In the beginning, mountains are mountains and rivers are rivers. Then mountains are no longer mountains, river are no longer rivers. Then there are no mountains or rivers. Finally, mountains are just mountains and rivers are just rivers."**

• **"Zen is chopping wood and carrying water."**

## Procedures at centers and temples

Zen centers and temples that follow a traditional Eastern model require practitioners to remove their shoes, change into slippers, and cover their street clothes with a robe. Sitting generally lasts at least half an hour, but may be interrupted by *kinhin* or "walking zazen," which is sometimes accompanied by the beating of a drum. At the end of each sitting session, a gong or handbell is sounded and practitioners rise slowly from their pillows to reenter daily life.

Services include the lighting of incense, the chanting of sutras, and prostration (bowing). Westerners who have been brought up in the Judeo-Christian tradition tend to look at bowing as a form of worship—which makes for discomfort when prostrating before statues of Buddha and Kannon (the Japanese name for the embodiment of Buddha as the most perfectly compassionate being). In the East, however, bowing is simply seen as a gesture of gratitude. Thus bowing before a statue of Buddha is not considered idol worship; rather, it is a way of showing gratitude to the historical Buddha (and to all those preceding and following him) for showing the way to Enlightenment. A different interpretation of bowing is known as the "lowering of the ego"—bringing the head down to the level of your belly, to remind you not to be ruled by your monkey-mind. Yet another view

### The "hitting stick"

In some more traditional centers and temples, members circulate through the sitters with *kyosaku* or "hitting sticks" to whack sitters who seem inattentive and/or unfocused. People can even ask to be hit with the kyosaku, because sometimes this has been known to induce satori. To some, this resembles sadomasochism, but different centers and temples have adopted different policies with regard to it, so make sure you find out.

**Above** Creative epiphanies are sometimes referred to as a whack on the side of the head. In some Zen temples, hitting sticks are used for precisely this reason (though not to the side of the head).

**Right** The influence of the Far East pervades many Zen temples. Slippers are worn indoors and incense is used to heighten the senses during zazen.

of prostration is that, by tipping yourself over, you are like a cup completely emptying itself of its contents, ready to be filled with the light of satori.

The cumulative effect of the incense, chanting, and prostration can be quite hypnotic—and to some people, this is the whole point. Much as people lose themselves in the beautiful fragrances and organ melodies of church services, so Zen students become immersed in an atmosphere that engages all the senses; this has a transformatory power and—occasionally—gives rise to satori all on its own.

Another element of center and temple services is the *teisho*, or lecture, which is given by the roshi, generally before the sitting itself. This is an opportunity for the roshi to remind practitioners of the basic tenets of faith, or simply to advise people on their sitting.

## Advantages of sangha practice

The advantages of belonging to a sangha are those of belonging to any spiritual community. Following a spiritual path is easier when surrounded by like-minded people, who can give encouragement and advice. Such groups provide a more complete "Zen experience"—an atmosphere that helps focus and still the mind, away from the distractions of home or work. Another plus is learning from more advanced students (not to mention the roshi), who can guide you through difficulties.

Centers and temples usually enjoy both informal and formal ties with other such communities in other cities; thus if you are traveling or moving elsewhere, people at your "home" sangha can usually refer you to practitioners at your destination, who will help you maintain and continue your practice.

> *" Nothing is born, nothing is destroyed. Away with your dualism, your likes and dislikes. Every single thing is just One Mind. When you have perceived this, you will have mounted the Chariot of the Buddhas. "*
>
> HUANG BO
> ZEN MASTER
> ?–849 C.E.

**Above** Bowing is a show of respect and gratitude—not abasement or worship. We bow to the Buddha to thank him for his insights; we bow to our roshi to thank him/her for helping us along the path to nirvana.

## Sesshin

Sesshin are retreats where practitioners can concentrate on attaining satori. During sesshin, adherents generally stay at a center or temple for their meals and sleep. Meals tend toward the simple and vegetarian, usually including rice and soup, and are prepared by sesshin members. In the larger temples and centers participants sleep and eat in sizeable common areas, which are cleaned regularly as part of daily practice. Retreats can range from overnight stays to weekends and week-long events. In the traditional sesshin, students are expected to remain for the entire time, unless a grave family emergency arises. Major centers and temples schedule at least one sesshin per year—and often more. Participants must register ahead of time and pay a small fee to cover their food and boarding costs.

One feature of Rinzai and hybrid sesshin is the dokusan, when individual students meet their roshi to discuss their personal "hunt for the ox." In the Rinzai tradition, students are also tested on their koans. Dokusan can be quite overwhelming, because students sit before the imposing master, who might whack them with a kyosaku or a fly-whisk to test their responses and thus their attainment of satori.

**Above** Meals at temple and during sesshin are usually sparse, often consisting of breakfast and a large lunch. Large meals dull the mind and cause drowsiness, interfering with zazen.

**Left** Buddhist monks are not allowed to take nourishment after noon or rest unless they have worked that day.

### The sesshin schedule

By their very nature, sesshin are intense. The typical day begins at around 4.30 A.M. with a sitting session, followed by a light breakfast, more sitting and lectures, a large lunch (considered the main meal of the day, for traditional Buddhists refrain from eating very much after lunch), more sitting, supper, and even more sitting into the night. Kinhin and teisho are interspersed, and students are urged to continue their practice even while preparing and eating meals, as well as performing whatever menial tasks are required during the sesshin.

## Freeing the mind

During sesshin, small talk, gossip, and other unnecessary verbiage are discouraged—and usually, after the second day or so, people are too focused on their practice to waste time in talk. Even formal greetings are dispensed with. Students are also admonished to keep their gaze on the floor as much as possible. This is meant to help students remain undistracted, which can be hard if the temple grounds are beautiful.

Traditional sesshin are therefore quite regimented and follow strict schedules. Some people might protest that such regimentation goes against the spirit of Zen; the response is that discipline frees the mind and spirit from worrying about details, allowing them to concern themselves with deeper, more spiritual questions.

### Sesshin innovations

Recently some sesshin have departed from the traditional model and taken advantage of the rising interest in ecological and adventure-based tourism. Sesshin are now taking place in remote, wilderness settings. Individuals are dropped at idyllic, isolated locations and then left to fend for themselves for a week. Naturally these sesshin are much more expensive, due to the costs of transportation. Other sangha have loosened up on the traditional rules of sesshin, allowing members to come and go as they please (their fee being proportional to the length of their stay). Again, the choice lies with you—and can only be made by trying out sesshin at different sangha and coming to your own conclusions.

> " To what should
> I liken the world?
> Moonlight, reflected
> in dewdrops,
> shaken from a crane's bill. "
>
> DOGEN ZEN MASTER
> FOUNDER OF THE SOTO SCHOOL
> 1200–1253

# Moving On
## 10 Questions & Answers

**Q** Should I allow the nature of my practice to change over time?

**A** "Should" and "shouldn't" are dualistic. If you sit zazen, sit zazen. Over time you may find that other activities provide natural vehicles for your practice. If so, follow them with focused attention.

**Q** Painting focuses my mind better than zazen. Should I stick with the zazen, or make painting my practice?

**A** You should consult your roshi, if you have one. She may recommend that you persist with zazen or go with painting. Ultimately, you can experiment both ways and see what works for you. Zen is good only as far as it conforms to your day-to-day life.

**Q** How do I decide if a particular center or temple is for me?

**A** Talk to the other members; talk to the roshi. Find out which lineage they follow, about their schedules for daily sittings, and about any sesshin that they offer. Sit with them two or three times and see how it feels. Follow your instincts.

**Q** I'm uncomfortable with bowing before statues. What can I do about this?

**A** Some centers and temples are open-minded about Westerners who associate bowing with idol worship. Talk to other members and to the roshi and get their feedback. You will either work through it or you won't.

**Q** Kyosaku really annoy me, but my center uses them. Is there anything I can do?

**A** Usually you can ask not to be hit with the kyosaku, but your feelings may persist nonetheless. Ask yourself, "Who is hitting? Who is being hit?"

**Q** I don't fit in at the Zen center in my area. What should I do?

**A** You can look for one further away or try to start one of your own. Avoid the politics that sometimes arise through discontent. Allow yourself, and others, the freedom to practice as you wish.

**Q** I have a local center that doesn't suit me and one far away, which does. Is the travel time worth it?

**A** Only you can decide this. If you must travel a long distance to get to your center, make travel itself your practice. In the long run, however, you might consider moving.

**Q** How often should I attend sesshin?

**A** Most serious adherents attend at least one sesshin a year—often more frequently. But sesshin are not obligatory.

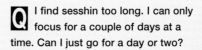

**Q** I find sesshin too long. I can only focus for a couple of days at a time. Can I just go for a day or two?

**A** Most centers and temples discourage leaving mid-sesshin (barring some unforeseen emergency). Leaving in the middle is disruptive and somewhat demoralizing to others. You can just go for two days by booking a weekend session. Have some consideration; if you can't hack more than a weekend, don't sign up for week-long sesshin.

**Q** I find sesshin too hard. Can I attain satori without them?

**A** There is no one road to satori. Sesshin are helpful to some, less so to others. The important thing is to maintain your practice.

# Glossary

**AWARE** Pathos, or the joy and sorrow of living.

**BODHI TREE** The tree under which Siddhartha sat and found Enlightenment.

**BODHISATTVA** An enlightened being that defers its exit from samsara in order to help others achieve nirvana.

**BUDDHA/BUDDHA** In the historical sense "Buddha" was the name given to Siddhartha Gautama when he achieved Enlightenment; literally, "one who is alive to the fundamental meaning of existence"—hence, anyone who has achieved Awakening.

**BUDDHA-NATURE** An object's essential essence or true nature.

**BUSHIDO** The warrior code of the samurai—a combination of Zen and traditional warrior ethics.

**CHANOYU** Literally "hot water for tea"—hence, the common name for the tea ceremony.

**CONFUCIANISM** A school of moral and religious philosophy founded by Confucius, or Kong Fuzi (551–479 B.C.E.), whose writings include the *Analects, Odes, Rights,* and the *Spring and Summer Annals*.

**DAOISM** A religion that sprang up around a book called the *Dao Dejing*, written—according to legend—by Laozi sometime during the fifth century B.C.E.

**DHARMA** The truth that Siddhartha experienced and passed on to his disciples; hence, the term for the teachings of Buddha.

**DOKUSAN** A testing personal interview between a roshi and a student, which usually occurs during a sesshin.

**DHYANA** A Sanskrit word referring to the meditative brand of Buddhism now known as Zen (or Chan in Chinese).

**ENSO** In calligraphy, a large monochrome circle painted in one stroke and surrounded by a commentary.

**GONG-FU** An unarmed Chinese martial art from which Japanese karetedo and *shurinji kenpo* are derived.

**HAIKU** An evocative Japanese poem made up of 17 syllables over three lines, with philosophical or spiritual overtones.

**HARA** The Japanese term for belly; also a person's spiritual center.

**IAIDO** The Japanese martial art of sword play.

**ICHI-GO, ICHI-E** The Japanese term for "one encounter, one opportunity."

**IKEBANA** The popular Japanese style of flower arranging, characterized by controlling nature indoors, within a formal setting.

**JODO** The Japanese martial art of stick fighting.

**KABUKI** Highly stylized Edo period (1608–1867) Japanese drama for the lower classes, compare with No.

**KAISEKI** Originally a term for heated flat stones used by the monks to assuage the hunger pains, now used to describe a formal meal style in Japan and the light meal given in a tea ceremony.

**KAMPAKU** A political ruler of Japan.

**KARATEDO** The Japanese martial art of weaponless fighting.

**KARMA** A tally of the positive and negative deeds that we accumulate over endless lifespans and which dictate our destiny in our next rebirth.

**KATA** A set pattern exercise performed in the martial arts of Japan.

**KENDO** The Japanese martial art of fencing with bamboo swords.

**KENSHO** A Japanese term for Awakening; an alternative term to satori.

**KINHIN** A round of ritualized walking, accompanied by the beating of a drum, during which students concentrate on placing one foot in front of the other.

**KOAN** A riddle whose solution may help the practitioner achieve a deeper state of consciousness.

**KYOSAKU** A "hitting stick" used at some traditional Zen centers and temples to whack sitters who appear unfocused.

**KYUDO** The Japanese martial art of archery.

**MANDALA** A circular symbol that represents the universe and acts as a focus for meditation.

**MAKYO** A distracting vision or illusion that frequently occurs during zazen.

**MONDO** A question-and-answer dialog between a Zen master and his or her disciple.

**MONO NO AWARE** A sense of finiteness, melancholy, loneliness, and emptiness.

**MU-SHIN** A Zen term meaning "no mind" describing a state of activity where experience and practice take over the actions of the body freeing the mind from concentrating on the activity.

**NIRVANA** A state of nothingness—having escaped suffering by exiting the cycle of life and death—whereby samsara is transcended.

**NO** A masked drama incorporating song, poetry, tragedy, sorrowful music, and dance, all heavily imbued with the Zen esthetic.

**ORIBE** Ceramic style in stoneware named after tea master Furuta Oribe, characterized by rough lines and heavy use of cutting of vessel edges, green and brown glazes used on a cream body.

**PALI** An ancient Indo-Aryan language used in the canonical books of Buddhists.

**PATRIARCH** One of the founding fathers of Buddhism.

**RAKU** A rough style of Japanese pottery characterized by "controlled" imperfections.

**RENGA** A poem consisting of linked-verse waka.

**RINZAI** A Japanese Zen school, founded in the twelfth century by Eisai and characterized by the use of koans to reach a deeper state of consciousness.

**ROSHI** A Zen master (male or, nowadays, female), who provides guidance and training for Zen students.

**SABI** A Japanese term that embodies serenity, melancholy, and loneliness.

**SADO** Literally, the "way of tea" or "tea-ism"—hence, the tea ceremony.

**SAKURA** Cherry blossom, the emblem of the samurai.

**SAMSARA** The endless cycle of death and rebirth to which beings in the material world are subjected until they attain nirvana.

**SAMURAI** A lord's retainer in feudal Japan, charged with bearing arms in support of their master during wartime and with keeping order in peacetime.

**SANGHA** A Buddhist community.

**SANSKRIT** An ancient Indo-Aryan language in which Buddhist texts were often written.

**SATORI** The state of Awakening or Enlightenment that all Buddhists seek ultimately to attain.

**SESSHIN** A Buddhist retreat at which practitioners concentrate on attaining satori.

**SHINGON BUDDHISM** Esoteric Buddhism, based on the premise of Enlightenment possible in the present world, through the addition of secret teachings, including mandala usage, ritual, mantra, and hand symbols (mudra).

**SHIKAN-TAZA** A state of all-round awareness, achieved by following the breath in and out of the nostrils, that is one of the highest levels of zazen.

**SHOGUN** One of the commanders-in-chief who effectively ruled Japan from the twelfth to the nineteenth century.

**SOTO** An austere Japanese Zen school, founded by Dogen in the thirteenth century.

**SUTRA** A Buddhist text or scripture.

**TABI** Socks, with thick soles and divisions for the big toes, that are worn with Japanese sandals.

**TATAMI** A rush-covered straw mat that forms a traditional Japanese floor covering.

**TATHAGATHA** He Who Has Traveled Forward and Returned—another name for the Buddha.

**TEISHO** A lecture given by a roshi before a sitting, to offer advice or to recap on the basic tenets of faith.

**THREE PRECEPTS** The precepts that the Buddha apprehended beneath the bodhi tree and which form the basis of Buddhism.

**UKIYO-E** A woodblock print.

**WABI** The Japanese term for something that blends with the elegance of the natural world.

**WABI-CHA** The style of tea ceremony derived from the merchant class in the late Civil War era (sixteenth century) and codified into the "modern" tea ceremony by Sen Rikyu in the late sixteenth century (as opposed to court tea styles of the Ashikaga period and before).

**WAKA** A Japanese poem of 31 syllables.

**YUGEN** The Japanese term for something that gives a glimpse into the Unfathomable.

**ZAFU** A traditional goose-down sitting cushion used in the practice of zazen, also *zabuton* in modern Japanese.

**ZAZEN** Literally, "sitting Zen"—the practice of "just sitting" that is one of the fundamentals of Zen practice.

# Further Reading

Austin, James H., *Zen and the Brain*, MIT Press, 1999.

Benoit, Hubert, *Zen and the Psychology of Transformation: The Supreme Doctrine,* Inner Traditions, 1990.

Campbell, Joseph, *Hero With a Thousand Faces*, Princeton University Press, 1972.

Fields, Rick, *How the Swans Came to the Lake: A narrative history of Buddhism in America,* Shambhala, 1992.

Gendlin, Dr. Eugene, *Focusing*, Bantam Books, 1982.

Goldberg, Natalie, *Writing Down the Bones*, Shambhala, 1986.

Herrigel, Eugen, *Zen in the Art of Archery*, Random House, 1999.

Kamenetz, Rodger, *The Jew in the Lotus*, Harper San Francisco, 1995.

Kapleau, Philip, *The Three Pillars of Zen: Teaching, Practice, and Enlightenment*, Harper and Row/Rider, 1980.

Kapleau, Philip, *Zen Dawn in the West*, Rider, 1980.

Kaye, Les, *Zen at Work*, Crown, 1997.

Kennedy, Father Robert E., *Zen Spirit, Christian Spirit*, Continuum, 1996.

Kerouac, Jack, *The Dharma Bums*, Penguin USA, 1991.

Kerouac, Jack, *On the Road*, Viking Press, 1997/Penguin USA, 1991.

Kettridge, William, *Owning It All,* Graywolf Press, 1988.

Lee, Anthony Man-tu, *Book of Zen Wisdom,* Barrons Educational Series, Inc., 2000.

Lee, Vinny, *Zen Interiors*, Stewart Tabori & Chang, 2000.

Orsborn, Carol, *How Would Confucius Ask For a Raise?*, William Morrow & Co., 1994.

Pirsig, Robert M., *Zen and the Art of Motorcycle Maintenance*, William Morrow & Co., 1974/Harperperennial Library, 2000.

Reps, Paul, and Senzaki, Nyogen (compiler), *Zen Flesh, Zen Bones*, Charles E. Tuttle, 1988. (To order call Tuttle's toll-free number: 1-800-526-2778.)

Shibayama, Zenkei, and Kodo, Sumido (trans.), *The Gateless Barrier: Zen Comments on the Mumonkan*, Shambhala, 2000.

Suzuki, Daisetz, *Essays in Zen Buddhism*, First Series: Grove Press, 1986; Second and Third Series: South Asia Books, 2000.

Suzuki, Shunryu, *Zen Mind, Beginner's Mind*, Weatherhill, 1970.

Tidbury, Jane, *Zen Style: Balance and Simplicity for Your Home*, Universe, 1999.

Watts, Alan, *The Way of Zen*, Grove Press, 1958.

# Useful Addresses

### BuddhaNet Buddhist Information Network— Gateway to Buddhism

http://www.buddhanet.net/

BuddhaNet™ is the result of a vision to link up with the growing worldwide culture of people committed to the Buddha's teachings and lifestyle.

### American Zen Association

New Orleans Zen Temple
748 Camp Street
New Orleans, LA
70130-3702

Phone: 504.523.1213
Fax:504.523.7024
aza@webdsi.com

www.gnofn.org/~aza/welcome.html

### Alt.zen newsgroup

http://www.ibiblio.org/zen/faq.html

A site containing Frequently Asked Questions about Zen.

### Zen Buddhism WWW Virtual Library

http://www.ciolek.com/WWWVL-Zen.html

Directs you to a multitude of information about Zen, including general resources, study pages, daily sutras, Zen documents, organizations, and so on.

### Zen Buddhism: *The Columbia Encyclopedia*, Sixth Edition, 2001:

http://www.bartleby.com/65/ze/ZenBuddh.html

### Religious Movements Homepage, Zen Buddhism:

http://religiousmovements.lib.virginia.edu/nrms/zen.html

Useful page containing information about Zen Buddhism with links.

### Zen Guide, The on-line guide to Zen and Buddhism— Concepts, Discussion, Community, and Resources

http://www.zenguide.com/

### Zen Stories to Tell Your Neighbors

http://www.dailyzen.com/

http://www.rider.edu/users/suler/zenstory/zenstory.html

### *History of Zen*

Page from Encarta Web encyclopedia about Buddha

http://encarta.msn.com/find/Concise.asp?z=1&pg=2&ti=761552413

Beat East meets West web site

http://www.bluesforpeace.com/beat_zen.htm

### The Precepts of Zen

Is Zen a Religion? by Kubota Jiun (translated by Paul Shepherd)

http://www.mkzc.org/kubisze.html

The Ten Oxherding Pictures

http://www.zip.com.au/~lyallg/tenbulls.htm

The 10 Bulls by Kakuan— transcribed by Nyogen Sentai and Paul Reps. Illustrated by Tomikichuro

Tokurikihttp://www.cs.sfu.ca/people/ResearchStaff/jamie/personal/10_Bulls/Title_Page.html

### Zen at Home

North Texas Institute for Educators on the Visual Arts—The Japanese Esthetic—A conversation with Jennifer Casler, Curator of Asian Art, Kimbell Art Museum

http://www.art.unt.edu/ntieva/artcurr/japan/inteπrvie.htm

### Zen at Work

The story of Les Kaye, IBM engineer, abbot of Mountain View Zen Meditation Center, and author of "Zen at Work"

http://www.execpc.com/~shepler/zen.html

The Zen of Your Home Office Space by Jeff Berner

http://www.myprimetime.com/work/life/content/zen8/index.shtml

Source of the lessons from "Tim" on Staten Island:

http://hometown.aol.com/TimKG/vadha.html

### Zen at Play

Zen samurai

http://www.keganpaul.com/features/zen_samurai.html

### Zen, the Self, and Others

Discussions on Zen, stories, terms, great reads, and lots of other Zen info.

http://www.yakrider.com/Buddha/Zen/Zen.htm

Information on focusing

http://www.focusingresources.com/articles/thoughtsonrad.html

Information on biofeedback

http://members.cts.com/crash/d/deohair/psychoph.html

Information on Naikan therapy

http://members.aol.com/naikanusa/whatis_english.html

Articles on Zen psychology or Buddhistic psychology

http://hanshananigan.tripod.com/zenid.html

# Index

## Acknowledgments

David would like to thank: his parents Joseph and Ruth, and brother Jonathan; Roshi Lee for getting the ball rolling; Nancy Steinhauer for being exactly who she is; Sophie Collins, Steve Luck, and Caroline Earle at Ivy Press for keeping the project alive and moving along; Crescent School for support and keeping the bills paid; and Kathy Rasmussen for taking care of Hazel.

Anthony would like to thank: David for all his hard work in bringing this project to fruition. Special thanks to my wife Glenda, my parents, and family. *Gate, gate, paragate, parasamgate, om svaha...*

## Picture credits

**CORBIS** 7T Kelly-Mooney Photographs, 8–9 Keren Su, 16–18 all Henry Ditz, 19BR Neal Preston, 22–23 Pat Jerrold/Paplio, 27 Ralph A.Clevenger, 34B Michael Freeman, 35R John Hulme/Eye Ubiquitous, 41 Michael S.Yamashita, 55T Michael Freeman, 60 Randy Faris, 63 Elizabeth Whiting Associates, 64 Lynn Goldsmith, 70–71 Janez Skok, 72 Robert Holmes, 73 Kelly-Mooney Photos, 74–75 and 77R and 78B Michael S Yamashita, 80T Craig Lovell, 80–81 Historical Picture Archive, 87 Dave Bartruff, 101 Michael S.Yamashita, 103 Bruce Burkhardt, 112–113 Paul Almasy, 116–117 Darrell Gulin, 118–119 Horace Bristol, 121 Richard T. Nowitz, 126 Darrell Gulin, 127 Don Hammond, 133 Cindy Kassab

**CORBIS / STOCKMARKET** p.98.

**GETTYONE / STONE** 12T Betsie Van der Meer, 20T Bruno Barbier, 26T Phil Borges, 43 Simeone Hubert, 46 Philip Lee Harvey, 82T Paul Chesley, 86 Robert Daly, 98BL Terry Husebye, 99BL Marc Dolphin, 107 Michael Wong

**GETTYONE / THE IMAGE BANK** 58–59 Core Agency, 62 Marc Romenelli, 76T, 81R Carlos Navajas, 89 Hans Neleman, 92–93 Tomek Sikora

**THE HUTCHISON LIBRARY** 14TR and 26B Michael Macintyre, 27 John Burbank , 47 Patricio Goycoolea, 68 Michael Macintyre, 114B and 131 Patricio Goycoolea, 132BL Michael Macintyre

**JAPAN NATIONAL TOURIST OFFICE** 130T